SEVEN DAYS A WEEK:
Faith in Action

Called to Holy Worldliness
by Richard J. Mouw

Christians with Secular Power
by Mark Gibbs

Thank God, It's Monday!
by William E. Diehl

Christian Maturity and Christian Success
by Daniel Jenkins

SEVEN DAYS A WEEK:
Faith in Action

Nelvin Vos

FORTRESS PRESS   **Philadelphia**

LAITY EXCHANGE BOOKS

The poem on p. 10 is by George Herbert. It was originally published in his posthumous *The Tingle* (1633) under the heading "Praise." The poem is taken from *Songs of Praise, Enlarged Edition,* edited by R. Vaughan Williams and Martin Shaw, Oxford University Press, 1931.

Biblical quotations, unless otherwise noted, are from the Revised Standard Version of the Bible, copyright 1946, 1952, © 1971, 1973 by the Division of Christian Education of the National Council of the Churches of Christ in the U.S.A. and are used by permission.

COPYRIGHT © 1985 BY FORTRESS PRESS

Library of Congress Cataloging in Publication Data

Vos, Nelvin.
    Seven days a week.

    (Laity exchange books)
    Adaptation and revision of: Monday's ministries.
    1. Christian life—Lutheran authors. 2. Lay ministry. I. Vos, Nelvin. Monday's ministries. II. Title. III. Title: 7 days a week. IV. Series.
BV4501.2.V64 1985   248.4'84133   84–47937
ISBN 0–8006–1658-8 (pbk.)

K983G84   Printed in the United States of America   1–1658

Contents

Editor's Introduction

THIS SERIES of Laity Exchange Books is intended above all to help the Christian laity develop their understanding of how we are called to serve and minister today. I am very happy that we can include in the series this book by Nelvin Vos, and for two reasons in particular.

In the first place, Nelvin has proved himself over the years as a sharp and distinguished advocate of the calling and the ministries of *all* the people of God. He is proud to be a Lutheran, and has worked with great energy to explore the rich potential of laypeople, especially in the Lutheran Church in America and in the organization LAOS in Ministry. He is to be admired for the skill he has shown in working in partnership with church leaders and professional theologians, and for his faithful persistence in all those necessary but often unexciting commissions and committees by which a great church is governed— and which are at this moment in history designing a greater Lutheran church for North America. He knows what he is writing about, both with his mind and with his heart.

But second: though he is skilled in the subtleties of theological debate, he is determined to speak and to write plainly and clearly. This is above all an admirable book for local church members, for parish groups, and for Christians struggling to make sense of their "high calling in Christ Jesus" in their ordinary lives and occupations. And his forthright teaching is not only for Lutherans, by any means. I am sure that very many Roman Catholics, Episcopalians, and Protes-

tants will find his approach attractively ecumenical, and a convincing
challenge to take our common faith into every aspect of our daily
lives.

MARK GIBBS

Preface

THIS BOOK is an adaptation and revision of *Monday's Ministries,* a study guide I wrote several years ago for the Division for Parish Services of the Lutheran Church in America. *Monday's Ministries,* with its leader guide and participant book, was written as a course in adult education. Positive response to it has encouraged me to accept the request to rework the material into a volume in the Laity Exchange series.

I have revised the format and the approach as well as several sections of the original course. Most of the revisions are based on learnings I acquired through participation in retreats and conferences on the ministry of the laity over the past five years.

Many books on the ministry of the laity are exhortatory and tend to talk *about* the subject. I have attempted here to address the many readers who already are working at relating faith and daily life. Although this book has been written with the individual reader in mind, it may also be used in group discussions.

I am grateful to the Division for Parish Services for permission to adapt and revise *Monday's Ministries* in this form. Raymond Tiemeyer of the Division deserves a special word of gratitude for helping make the original *Monday's Ministries* course both clear and lively. Finally, I wish to thank Ms. Christine Fiedler, whose skill in tracing sources was invaluable, and especially Mrs. Dorothy Jones, whose careful typing and constant encouragement were a ministry of support to me in the task.

Seven whole days, not one in seven,
I will praise thee;
In my heart, though not in heaven,
I can raise thee.
Small it is, in this poor sort
to enrol thee:
E'en eternity's too short
to extol thee.

PART ONE

CALLED TO MINISTER

1

Connecting Faith and Life

WHAT CHALLENGED YOU this past week? What haunted or bugged you? What sustained you, gave you joy? What tensions were present? At which of these points and in what ways did your daily living intersect with your Christian faith? How did the realities of your daily living (pressure, tensions, competition, success, compromise, conflict) relate to the realities of your faith (prayer, the presence of God)?

Such questions come to each of us out of the hustle and bustle of our daily lives. Some days we can ignore these questions or take them for granted; other times the questions are directly before us or haunt us. Yet the fundamental question is always there: How is what we do and how we live connected to our faith?

These particular words are important about our faith and daily life: intersect, relate, connect. Others could be added: bridge, integrate, link, meet. What they all imply is a putting together, a unifying of our faith and action, our commitment and our practice. They all imply an "and," that little word which is one of the most important we hear and use.

I once heard the Swiss theologian Karl Barth say: "'And' is one of the most interesting and difficult words in language: heaven and earth, male and female, God and man." I would add faith *and* daily life.

This book will attempt to *evoke* those connections between your faith and daily life which you already recognize, to *encourage* and *support* you in realizing fuller and richer ways to bridge each of those gaps we sometimes sense, and to *equip* you to be still more effective in living your life from a faith stance.

In one sense, such talk of intersecting, connecting, and relating faith and daily life is misleading. It assumes that there are two separate realms: faith and daily life. It acts as if there are two entities—God and world—which depend on us to put the two together.

But we do not have two separate lives, that is, a spiritual life and the remaining part of our life. In fact, our faith commitment is frequently so entangled in mundane affairs that we do not know where the one begins and the other ends. The question, Should I connect faith and life? is therefore almost as absurd as, Should the fish be in the pond? The real point is not whether, but how—how to become more fully aware of the connections between faith and life.

To Be in Ministry

One word catches the essence of what it means to see our total life as a faith commitment. That word is ministry.

The root sense of the word "minister" is to be minor, to be less, to give help to others, to be a servant, or as might be said in today's language, to be a waitress or a waiter. Jesus, at about age thirty-three, an itinerant teacher, might have said something like this: "Whoever would be great among you must be your waiter. I came not to be waited on but to be a servant."

"If one of you wants to be great, he must be the servant of the rest; and if one of you wants to be first, he must be your slave—like the Son of man, who did not come to be served, but to serve and to give his life to redeem many people" (Matt. 20:26–28, TEV).

Ministry is not limited to certain persons, places, and times; ministry is God acting through the whole people of God for the life of the world in every time and place. It is exercised both in the daily service that Christians offer to one another and to the world and in the proclamation of the Word and the administration of the sacraments. In ministry, the people of God respond to the summons to be agents of God for bringing "all things in heaven and earth together under one head, even Christ" (Eph. 1:10).

Ministry is shaped by the unique ministry of the crucified and risen Christ. Jesus began his ministry where people were, not where he hoped they were or wanted them to be. He responded to their needs, which is illustrated in his compassion for the woman caught in adultery. She was extremely vulnerable. The stones might have killed her, and so could have words. He recognized a sinner, but saw beyond her weakness to a person capable of being saved. His forgiving hand gave her hope while touching this woman's need to be loved and to be one with God again. No wonder Jesus said that forgiveness and reconciliation are the surest signs of his living presence.

Ministry is the serving and witnessing we do where we are. Ministry is not something we go out and do, but rather something we do as we go. It takes place in the normal flow of daily events. We do not have to find our ministry; it finds us.

Ministry is not over there; it is here, where I am.

The world is not out there; it is in here, all around me.

Therefore, two very important questions in understanding our faith in daily life are: Where am I? Where do I minister?

In order to answer these questions, you might spend a few minutes responding to the following.

Ministry: Who and Where You and I Are

1. Describe your main daily activity—what you do and where you do it.
2. About how many persons do you meet in an average day?
3. About how many of these persons do you "minister" to in an average day? (You may define "minister" in as broad or narrow a sense as you wish.)
4. How do you minister to these persons?
5. List at least three kinds of decisions you make in your daily activity.
6. Does your Christian faith affect your decisions? How?
7. How could you be better equipped and supported in your ministry in the world?

Your answers to these questions can help you realize that you are already in ministry. Our ministry of service is not something extra we ought to be doing. It is something we are already doing!

My point is that ministry does not involve doing a great deal that is new and more difficult. Rather, it is working through some of the problems we already face and being aware of what we intend. By focusing on the here and now, we can attempt to bridge the gap between Sunday and Monday, between faith and family life, church and business. The meaning of life is either lost or found in our daily routines. To see the presence of God in daily life, to be the body of Jesus Christ there, and to feel nourished by the Holy Spirit there, is to find the meaning and the ministry.

Total Ministry

Ministry helps make sense of our lives. It is not something added to our Christian living, but something that unifies and connects what is already there. Even the roots of the words "connection" (*com-*, "together," and *nectere*, "to fasten") and "religion" (*re-*, "back," and *ligare*, "to bind," "to bind together") are parallel. Both words assume a quest for unity, for wholeness. Thus, our religion is a binding together of what already is. One's faith is that which integrates, unifies, makes sense of that which already is one's life.

In the biblical images, ministry is the salt or the leaven which permeates life. Lives that evidence a Spirit-filled dimension do so unconsciously as well as consciously. We are not in the Spirit only in those rare moments when we are aware of the presence of the Spirit. The Spirit is there in all we do. Life is not just a long series of gaps joined together by special spiritual exercises. We are the body of Christ, his ministers on earth, at all times.

We tend to be unaware of our ministries because we think 11:00 A.M. Sunday morning is God's time, 11:00 A.M. Monday morning is company time, and 11:00 P.M. Monday evening is our time. Or we divide our lives into spaces: this is the church and therefore this is holy space; that is a golf course and therefore that is recreational space. Such an approach is what news magazines do; they see religion as a slice of life. Religion is one fragment of our life, one compartment among others such as education, law, and sports.

Such compartmentalization is a reflection of a kind of modern religious schizophrenia. God is not believed to be present in certain times and places: Sunday morning, yes, of course, but not on Monday in my business or on Saturday in my recreation and leisure. God may be present in my decision making about the use of my income, but not in my political or sexual decisions. God may be present in the shop of the independent storekeeper, but not in the corporate boardroom or the union hall. God may be present with the nurse and the teacher, these helping professionals, but what about the UPS truck driver or the boy pumping gas? Of course, God is present in the beauty of the sunset and in the walk by the seashore, but what about in the grime of the factory or in the hectic tension of the computer center? Church spires point to the heavens, but what about the skyscraper of glass or the garish neon of used-car lots and fast-food places?

And so the schizophrenia grows. The world is, at worst, the domain of evil and endless confusion; at best, the world is neutral. We may sing "This is my Father's world" and "Beautiful Savior, King of Creation" with great vitality, but that is not the way it strikes us on Monday morning. Out of fear, vulnerability, and a deliberate protecting of self we believe too frequently in the doctrine of Christ's real presence at the altar and in the doctrine of Christ's real absence at the desk and assembly line and the kitchen sink.

And at the same time, a deep hunger comes through, a hunger to live all of life in the light of the Christ whom we confess. To see the wholeness of one's commitment to Christ, to be open to the Spirit wherever one is, and to be aware of the Creator in all the places one frequents—all these become steps on the journey to understand that all of creation, all of the earth, all of the world, is the Lord's. For Christ loves us wherever we are, and his love can be manifest in whatever we do. All time and space are of God.

Shared Ministry

Ministry takes places between people. We cannot be Christian by ourselves, and there can be no ministry apart from community.

"And so we shall all come together to that oneness in our faith and in our knowledge of the Son of God; we shall become mature people, reaching to the very height of Christ's full stature" (Eph. 4:13, TEV).

Our ministry not only gives love and support; it needs the love and support of a community of Christians around us and behind us. The community may range from one's spouse to the family to a small group expressly formed to support our ministry in the world to the entire congregation. No matter what the community, all such expressions reflect the fact that we share in God's ministry. In Pentecost the Spirit took separate human beings and overcame their estrangement.

"You were baptized into union with Christ, and now you are clothed, so to speak, with the life of Christ himself. So there is no difference between Jews and Gentiles, between slaves and free men,

between men and women; you are all one in union with Christ Jesus''
(Gal. 3:27-28, TEV).

We do not minister alone, but our very ministry in the name of Jesus
Christ relates us to and unites us with one another. Mutuality and
interdependence are the marks of shared ministry.

We are ministers because Christ ministers through us. We are not
ministers because we need to make ourselves good. Others can
quickly detect when we are serving them only because we want to
improve our standing with God or demonstrate goodness. That is a
personal moralism which can turn into a self-righteous pride and hurt
the ministry of Christ. Rather, our ministry is Christ acting through
us—often in small, humble, unnoticed ways—to bring health to the
world.

We are ministers because Christ has ministered to us. We are not
ministers because we are better people. We cannot boast of ethical
righteousness or deeper insights or stronger will. We can simply be
grateful that Christ wants to heal and help the world and wants to do
that through us—through any of us.

We are ministers because of Christ's love, not because of laws. The
ministry is not a code of behavior we are to follow. In fact, we cannot
even set up a code that tells us exactly what we are to do to serve in
each situation in which we minister. We cannot arrive at a predeter-
mined procedure and then impose it on ourselves or others. We can
only be ready to love and to work for justice. We may study the gospel
in advance, but its applicaton in any particular situation must be
developed within that situation. The need will dictate the way to
respond in service, witness, or prophecy.

Thus ministry is the service which all people share with one another
and the world, but which Christians especially share because of the
ministry that Jesus Christ performs for them and through them. This is
a responsibility and a privilege given to all Christians, not just to a few
who are ordained. There is only one ministry, the ministry of God
himself working through engineers and nurses, pastors and plumbers,
farmers and secretaries, homemakers and teachers. Every member of
the body of Christ is a minister. Each of us is called in Jesus' name to
serve God's people and his world.

The whole ministry is given to the whole church for the whole
world.

2

How in the World
Are You Doing?

Yes, how in the world *are* you doing? That is a good question for us to ask one another, not in judgment, but in support and encouragement. For it is in the world that we are called to minister.

We are not here to transcend the world, but to live fully in it with God's presence. The way to God is not first of all up to the heavens, but down to the depths of life. A Christian is a person who really lives, who is fully involved in the activities of the world around us.

We are called in the intersections where our faith in Jesus Christ meets and confronts the concreteness of daily living: in making decisions, in relating to others, in doing justice within our communities, in working to change the corporate structures of society, in being part of a global network of interrelationships. In all of these arenas we are sustained and strengthened by the knowledge that God has called us out of darkness into marvelous light.

And yet the people of God often do not see themselves as the church. Recently, a participant in a retreat in faith and daily life, which I happened to be leading, told of a church member who was reporting to a church council meeting on a Fair Housing Task Force in a medium-sized midwestern city. The member, as chairperson of the social ministry committee, recounted the struggling and wrestling going on at the downtown session. He said that government and city officials as well as local lobbyists were present, and then looking directly at the pastor added, "But the church was not there." Another member of the council finally broke the silence: "But you were there, Ed! You are the church! You know the housing problems in this city;

you have a deep commitment to your faith. You are the only church there is!''

The Whole Church Is the Body of Christ in the World

The church exists not for itself, but for and on behalf of the world. We are called, all of us, to be the salt of the earth, not to be the salt of the salt. Only when the church is not an end in itself is it faithful to Jesus Christ. A truck driver at a LAOS in Ministry retreat, which I led last spring, put it well in our last session together: ''I guess what I've learned this weekend is that I always thought I was in the world to go to church; now I see what I should have seen a long time ago, that I'm in the church in order to go into the world.''

To curve in on oneself—that is sin not only for individuals but also for institutions, including the church. Congregational report forms that inquire only of numerical increases of dollars and bodies and do not raise the question, How *in the world* are you doing? or pastors who act as if the parish is their world rather than the world is their parish, or laypeople who think that meaningful Christian ministry can take place only in church buildings, or seminarians who enter *the* ministry because in their previous so-called secular activity they did not feel they were ''in full-time Christian service''—in such particulars, the body of Christ distorts its mission. We must help one another to be liberated from the captivity of the institution turning in on itself. We tend to exalt those who do church work in the sense of institutional involvement more than those who are out there doing church work, which is the church at work, the body of Christ in the world. The church building is not first of all a shrine or an assembly hall, but in Elton Trueblood's words, the church building is the ''headquarters'' of the army of the committed.[1] The building in its worship, education, and fellowship is the base of operations. The field is the world.

As the body of Christ, we are to make Christ's presence real in the world. There will be no concerned Christ who heals and forgives and loves and liberates unless each of us, in the name of Christ, is concerned and heals and forgives and loves and liberates.

Every member of the body represents the body of Christ. The body of Christ is meant to be seen and heard and touched in ordinary places: the home, classroom, office, factory, store, and street. This is the world God so loved as to send the only-begotten Son, and it is to this beloved and bleeding world that God sends the church.

Our Monday World

We recognize the responsibility of all Christians to be the people of God in our Monday worlds. To engage in the ministry of the laity in the Monday world is to live one's Christian faith in every time and place where one is. That is where the encounter between the gospel and the world takes place.

The Christian faith is not for spectators who only want to listen to professionals, nor for individuals who want to seek their souls alone. It is made up of many people, all called to serve together as representatives of Christ in the world.

The ministry of the laity has been classified as:

1. The laypeople *in* the church (such as church school, choir).
2. The laypeople *through* the church (such as missions, institutions).
3. The laypeople *in the world* (such as farm, school, government).

We will concentrate on number three, ministry in the world. We will also recognize the importance of the second and first classifications, and later we will discuss the relationship between the ministry of the clergy and the ministry of the laity. But the emphasis will be on ministry in the world, because this is the area in which 99 percent of the people of God spend 90 percent of their time in an average week. This is where the church lives. This is where we encounter the tensions and challenges of life.

We will use the term "ministry of the laity" instead of "lay ministries." Lay ministries usually refers to specific functions such as the ministries of deacons or full-time lay professional church workers. The word "lay" sometimes implies untrained, inexperienced, even immature and second-rate. A second-rate ministry has no more validity than does an unskilled practice of law or medicine. The term "ministry of the laity" on the other hand, emphasizes that all Christians have a ministry, a service to perform. In fact, almost all of the ministry has to be done by the laity, because they are the ones who carry out the work of the Monday world.

One of the documents of the Second Vatican Council spoke of the role of the laity in the world:

By reason of their special vocation, it belongs to the laity to seek the kingdom of God by engaging in temporal affairs and directing them according to God's will. They live in the world, that is, they are engaged in each and every work and business of the earth and in the ordinary circumstances of social and family life which, as it were, constitute their very existence.[2]

God's ministry to us is real because it comes to us through people in the real world.

The Creation: Where We Are

I would submit that the church needs to underline the doctrine of creation (where we are).

The biblical understanding is that the creation as such is good. The created world is not a lower order of being but is itself the instrument of divine goodness. When God now chooses to reveal himself, he does so in and through the creation. The finite is capable of revealing the infinite. For creation refers to the way God brings order out of chaos and governs his world and makes it possible for us to live together in community. The whole creation is upheld by the Word of God. God is throbbingly alive in his world.

The world is the arena for our ministry, for our various callings. The whole earth is the Lord's and there is no sacred and secular division. Try a simple experiment sometime. Ask Christians to select photographs that show God's presence. The choices will be, more likely than not, soaring mountains and idyllic streams. But God is a God not only of nature, but also of history. The seemingly ordinary and the allegedly mundane in which women and men cultivate fields, design computer programs, empty bedpans, and vacuum carpets—this world is the locus of where we are in God's creation and where we are to be participants in the ongoing and interdependent work of his creation.

The world, the arena of God's activity, always speaks with ambiguity and opaqueness. That means motives are mixed; compromises must be struck. Yet it is in the very stuff of life that God calls us to be partners and colleagues—to participate in the care and nurture of our life together as humankind in creation. You and I are already part of God's intricate network of creation.

For the Christian there is nothing more spiritual or holy about going to church than there is about going to work. God comes to us in both places. As Christians, we are not called to leave behind body, money, work, amusement, politics. We are called upon to see these things as creations of God given to us to use them with him. Christianity is a down-to-earth approach. William Temple had it right: the line of penetration runs from the altar and pulpit to the pew to the pavement.

NOTES

1. Elton Trueblood, *The Company of the Committed* (New York: Harper & Row, 1961), 72–75.
2. Austin Flannery, O.P., ed., *Vatican Council II, The Conciliar and Post Conciliar Documents* (copyright 1975), chap. IV, art. 31. The document in its entirety may be obtained from the Publications Office of the United States Catholic Conference, 1312 Massachusetts Ave. N.W., Washington, D.C. 20005.

3

The People of God:
Priests with a Vocation

"THE PEOPLE of God"—these four simple words contained perhaps the most dramatic idea in church history in the twentieth century. For these four words are used as the controlling image of *Lumen Gentium*, the Dogmatic Constitution on the Church set forth by the Second Vatican Council. Instead of opening with a discussion of the structure and government of the church—as Vatican I did—chapter 1, "The Mystery of the Church," begins with the ringing note, "Christ is the light of the nations," and goes on to speak of the church as the people to whom God communicates himself in love. The groundwork is then laid for devoting the second chapter to the description of the church as "the new people of God." This term refers to the total community of the church, including pastors as well as other faithful. A later chapter in *Lumen Gentium* speaks directly to those who

by their very vocation seek the kingdom of God by engaging in temporal affairs and by ordering them according to the plan of God. They live in the world, that is, in each and in all of the secular professions and occupations. They live in the ordinary circumstances of family and social life, from which the very web of their existence is woven.

They are called there by God so that by exercising their proper function and being led by the spirit of the gospel they can work for the sanctification of the world from within, in the manner of leaven. In this way they can make Christ known to others, especially by the testimony of a life resplendent in faith, hope, and charity.[1]

The entire spirit of the Second Vatican Council is permeated with the sense of the church as the people of God in mission and service in and to the world. Two later documents, "Pastoral Constitution on the

Church in the Modern World'' and ''Decree on the Apostolate of the Laity,'' spell out specific dimensions of what it means to be the people of God in today's world.

Such an understanding of the church is also reflected in the crucial opening sentence of the discussion on ministry in *Baptism, Eucharist and Ministry,* the Lima Report of the World Council of Churches: ''In a broken world God calls the whole of humanity to become God's people.''[2]

Some twenty years earlier, in 1961 at the New Delhi Assembly, the World Council of Churches had said:

> There is an urgent need for all Church members to recover the true meaning of certain words: to learn that the laity is really the ''Laos,'' that is, the whole People of God in the world, including, of course, those who have been ordained; to learn that ministry means any kind of service by which a Christian exercising his particular skill and gift, however humble, helps his fellow Christians or his fellow men in the name of Christ. A far richer fellowship and team spirit is bound to appear as soon as the whole Church comes to realize its function as the People of God, which God himself has provided with many kinds of ministry, in which one special kind of ministry, that of the ordained clergy, is set apart to strengthen and teach, to encourage and unite all the several witnesses in their various callings whose ministry is set in the heart of the secular world's manifold activity.[3]

Using the phrase ''the people of God'' instead of the terms ''laity'' and ''clergy'' to describe the church has far-reaching implications. The oneness and the wholeness of the ministry of the church is emphasized, for all of us as the people of God are called out and called forth.

To Be the Laity

Most of all, the term ''the people of God'' recovers the biblical perspective. In the Greek, *Laos* means ''people,'' not amateurs. The New Testament believers would be surprised to find only a part of the present Christian community designated as laity. To them, the word *laos* referred to all the people of God. The term ''clergy'' came second, not first. It was used to indicate which of the laity were given certain functions, not which of the people were not clergy.

The central text is 1 Pet. 2:9–10:

But you are a chosen race, a royal priesthood, a holy nation, God's own people, that you may declare the wonderful deeds of him who called you out of darkness into his marvelous light. Once you were no people but now you are God's people; once you had not received mercy but now you have received mercy.

Each time the word "people" is used, the Greek root is *laos*. All the people were the laity, with no distinction of office or responsibility.

Different persons, of course, had different gifts and different functions, even in the early Christian community:

And his gifts were that some should be apostles, some prophets, some evangelists, some pastors and teachers, to equip the saints for the work of ministry, for building up the body of Christ. (Eph. 4:11–12)

But all of the people had gifts, and all were of one status with all of the functionaries we now call clergy. All made up one union. The people were *all together* the people of God.

Many commentators have pointed out that this situation soon changed. They suggest that the distinction between clergy and laity had its source in civil affairs. In the Greco-Roman city-state, *laos* meant the citizens and *kleros* referred to the magistrates. This duality was carried over into the Christian community. Those who had a special office, those who *ad-ministered* the means of grace, became the *kleros* (clergy), and the bulk of the believers became the *laos*.

By the twelfth century a lawyer named Gratian said that there were two kinds of Christians. He was referring to clergy and laity. The meaning of *laos* as "all the people of God" had been lost. What was at stake was not just a matter of power and governance, but responsibility and service. By letting the clergy be the sole ministers, the laity lost their privileges and abdicated their responsibilities. They began to view themselves as second-class Christians who delegated their ministries to special persons called pastors and priests.

Herman Stuempfle aptly calls this development a "split level church":

On the lower level, exposed to all the dirt and grime of the world, their salvation always in jeopardy, totally dependent upon ministrations from above them, were the laity. On the upper level, closer to heaven, infused with divine grace, sheltered from the corruptions of the evil world, dispensing the medicine of the sacraments to the laity beneath them, were the clergy. Though the laity were by far the more numerous, there was by now no question that they were also the inferior sub-species of the genus Christian. A strange structure had arisen upon the New Testament foundations.[4]

This understanding of the Christian community is what the Reformers disputed. Stuempfle goes on to describe the kind of structure which the Reformers believed was biblical:

> The Reformation blueprint called for a church in which all Christians lived on one level. Certainly they didn't all occupy one room. There were various "office spaces." But none stood higher than any other, either in terms of nearness to God or of shelter from sin, death and the devil. Clergy were to be seen as distinct from the laity only in terms of function, not in terms of standing before God.[5]

Several theological understandings of the laity were affirmed by the Reformers as they struggled with the way in which Christians should see their relationship to God and to their neighbors. We will focus on two of these understandings: the priesthood of the baptized and the calling or vocation of the Christian.

To Be a Priest

If you were asked, Are you . . .

—a believer? You would probably answer, "Of course, I have faith."

—a disciple? You would surely say, "Yes, I follow the way of Christ."

—a minister? You would probably be a bit more hesitant, but you would probably say, "Yes, I attempt to serve others."

—a priest? Would you say, "Why, no, not really. They had priests long ago in Israel, but not today except in certain churches, and they are supposed to be different, aren't they?"

We can be candid among ourselves as to why we may find it difficult to say we are priests. False modesty, latent anti–Roman Catholicism, fear of what the responsibilities may entail, and other obstacles may stand in our way.

The term "priest" has carried much historical baggage which is still present today. In certain religious traditions, the priest is granted considerable status and privilege. In other traditions, the priest is not supposed to have special status, only special functions. In still other faiths, those functions are granted to all.

Both biblical thinking and theological history tell us that you and I *are* priests. A priest is a mediator, a bridge, and every Christian is a bridge between other people and God. God works through all people, both clergy and laity, to bring God and other people together.

When the Reformers emphasized the priesthood of all believers, they were referring to at least three characteristics:

We are priests for one another. Every person stands before God on behalf of others. Luther wasn't doing away with priests. He was saying that each of us is a priest to others. We represent others before God in prayers, and we represent God before others in forgiveness and deeds. That is the intercessory role of each of us as priests: to see in every creature someone for whom God cares, someone for whom I pray and serve. Such relationships between human beings make God's forgiving presence more personal.

Every believer is a priest. Every person may also stand before God directly, with only Christ as a go-between. The Reformers insisted that the Scriptures taught that every person has access to God and his Word. Certainly, confession and prayer in the presence of an ordained priest or a pastor or another person may be a means God uses to reveal his forgiveness, but such persons are not the only route to God. Every Christian stands in unmediated and unbroken relationships to God through Jesus Christ.

The whole church is a priest. The whole church is a priesthood, and you and I are part of that priesthood. We are priests with one another. Without that, we are isolated individuals, and the result of that is a self-centered piety. Not only is the church a corporate priesthood for its own members, but it stands as a priest between God and the world. It prays for the world and brings the love and care of God to the world.

To be a priest, therefore, involves both vertical and horizontal dimensions. Vertically, to be a priest implies the privilege of direct access to God. Horizontally, to be a priest emphasizes the responsibility to share the gospel by meeting one's neighbor in reconciling love and caring ministry. Such mediation and reconciliation include listening to the cries of human pain in one's place of involvement, attempting to heal those hurts, and discerning expressions of God's grace in those circumstances.

The Reformers rooted their thinking in the Old Testament teaching about the royal priesthood. The people of Israel were to be a "kingdom of priests'' (Exod. 19:6), a people particularly set apart to be God's servants. Every member of the kingdom of priests was privileged to draw near to God in dedication, worship, and service, so that they might learn how their mission to the world was to be fulfilled. These privileges belonged to the Lord's people as a community of believers and not to any particular individual or exclusive class of specialists. The people of Israel were called to be priests and to perform a distinctive service on God's behalf. God established a corporate covenant with the people of Israel which affirmed this mediating function. He graciously offered his steadfast love and redeeming action to this scraggly nation of cast-off slaves which he had called to himself.

In the New Testament, God himself fulfilled the priesthood in Jesus. The Son of God opened a new and living way between the world and God. A nonprofessional lay carpenter gave his body as a single sacrifice. In Jesus, God served and perspired and suffered.

The action of God in Christ came to a focus when the layperson bent to scrub feet. The Creator of all that exists took to himself a towel and sloshed water on the road-dirty disciples:

> When he had washed their feet, and taken his garments, and resumed his place, he said to them, ''Do you know what I have done to you? You call me Teacher and Lord; and you are right, for so I am. If I then, your Lord and Teacher, have washed your feet, you also ought to wash one another's feet. For I have given you an example, that you also should do as I have done to you. Truly, truly, I say to you, a servant is not greater than his master; nor is he who is sent greater than he who sent him. (John 13:12–16)

He took the form of a servant, and he called his followers to be servants, knee benders, dealers in dusty stuff.

Through the sweat and the blood of that Servant, the bending Priest, God called into being a new community. A new people was called to spread the good news of Christ's sacrifice for humanity. A new priesthood was created to carry on the suffering action of the one Mediator between God and human beings.

This was the charter of the church: the suffering service of the Lord. This was its only purpose for being: to mediate in menial ways with the world and for the world toward God.

You and I as baptized members of Christ's body are therefore members of that holy and royal priesthood (1 Pet. 2:5,9). The Revelation to John speaks several times of the redeemed as those "from every tribe and tongue and people and nations, and [whom God] hast made . . . a kingdom and priests to our God" (Rev. 1:5–6; 5:9–10; 20:6).

The task of the priest as God's servant and minister in the world is to do the work of reconciliation, to help to restore amid the brokenness. Both the ministry and the message of reconciliation are given to us, according to the writer of 2 Corinthians:

> Therefore, if any one is in Christ, he is a new creation; the old has passed away, behold, the new has come. All this is from God, who through Christ reconciled us to himself and gave us the ministry of reconciliation; that is, in Christ God was reconciling the world to himself, not counting their trespasses against them, and entrusting to us the message of reconciliation. (2 Cor. 5:17–19)

Jesus explained that, as priests, our prayers are heard by God:

> In that day you will ask in my name; and I do not say to you that I shall pray the Father for you; for the Father himself loves you, because you have loved me and have believed that I came from the Father. (John 16:26–27)

In one of his writings, Luther picks up on these verses:

> Here he has crowned, ordained, and anointed us all with the Holy Spirit so that all of us together are priests in Christ, exercise a priestly office, come before God and intercede for one another. Thus all of us may say, "Christ has become the high priest and he has prayed for me and gained for me faith and the Spirit; for this reason I am also a priest and should continue to pray for the people of the world that God would also give faith to them."[6]

I ask again: Are you a priest? May your answer be: "Yes, by God's grace, I offer myself to assist in God's work of mediation and reconciliation in the world."

To Be Called

But am I called? Do I have a vocation?

In order to answer these questions, we must recognize that vocation is a term which has undergone one metamorphosis after another.

The word itself is the Latin equivalent *(vocatio)* which the New Testament speaks of as *klesis,* that is, calling. The nuances of the term include at least two meanings: (1) to *summon* (often by name), to convoke an assembly; and (2) to *choose,* to select or assign to an office or a task. The biblical emphasis at all times is on the God who calls. And the response is God's called-out and called-forth people.

In the Scriptures, vocation is essentially corporate. God calls a people. In the Old Testament this people, this community, is Israel. Many times Israel would rather not have been the chosen one, for the burden of obedience and responsibility was heavy. Yet Israel could not escape its relationship to God. Israel was the chosen community of faith whom God summoned together for his service.

Within the community of Israel, individuals were chosen for specific tasks. The calls of Moses (Exodus 3–4), of Samuel (1 Samuel 3), of Isaiah (chap. 6), and of Jeremiah (chap. 1) were regarded not as a source of pride and honor but rather as a summons to particular service.

Jesus called twelve disciples at the beginning of his ministry. In Jesus Christ, the Word came among us. The call to live in the midst of the cross and the empty tomb is the summons for the new community, the church. Hence, the church itself was appropriately described as *ekklesia,* the assembly of those summoned into and chosen for the body of Christ.

In Paul, the meanings of calling are rich and varied: (1) the general summons from God to each man and woman to the life of faith and love (Rom. 8:28–30; 1 Cor. 1:1–2; 2 Thess. 2:13–14); (2) God's choosing or election of each believer within the corporate body of the church (1 Thess. 2:11–12; Eph. 4:1); (3) the particular summons to specific tasks within the community of faith (Rom. 1:1; 1 Cor. 1:1; Gal. 1:15–17); and (4) the earthly station of the Christian, allotted by divine will (Eph. 4:1–4; 1 Cor. 7:17–24). And in a crescendo of all four themes, Paul in 1 Corinthians 12 and Ephesians 4 describes the newly called community as one in Christ but manifesting itself in a rich variety of callings. For when Paul refers to apostles, prophets, evangelists, pastors, and teachers, and connects their ministry with the building up of the body of Christ, he is thinking in far greater dimensions than building up local congregations or even forming new church structures.

The biblical witness comes with an all-encompassing vision: the call of God addresses the whole of life. To each believer the Holy Spirit gives tasks appropriate to the calling and capacities needed for their accomplishment. There is one vocation for all, to serve Christ and the neighbor, yet each has distinctive work to do.

Robert L. Calhoun, Yale University historian, has traced in detail the metamorphoses of the term "vocation" in the early church.[7] Although the writings of the early church show evidence of discussing the first three Pauline dimensions of vocation, the fourth meaning of the earthly station of the Christian came to symbolize "the status of one seeking perfection."[8] The eventual result was the widespread acceptance of a double standard of Christian living: for ordinary Christians, obedience to the commandments; for the seekers of perfection, the contemplative life and the vows of poverty and celibacy. Monasticism (the life set apart from the world) and mysticism (the effort to see God directly) were clearly paths to perfection. Thus the monk, the priest, the nun had a calling. Other Christians had no vocation in the world.

The bold claim of Luther in recovering the biblical witness was twofold: (1) instead of priests limited to religious orders, as we saw earlier, all believers are priests; and (2) instead of one vocation (the calling of the religious orders), all Christians have a vocation. All are called in their baptism to live in the light of Christ's death and resurrection. Daily living is the arena of one's vocation, as Luther writes:

> You may reply: But how if I am not called? Answer: How is it possible that you are not called? You have always been a husband or wife, a boy or girl, or servant. . . . Again: Are you a prince, a lord, spiritual or secular who has more to do than you, in order that your subjects may do right, preserve peace, and wrong is done by no one? . . . See, as now no one is without some commission or calling.[9]

Note that in each of these terms, priests and vocation, Luther not only reinstituted biblical language but also appropriated the very words that had been used exclusively for religious orders. He insisted that the gracious call of the gospel and the promise of being justified by faith alone meant that all Christians at all times and places were priests with vocations.

The biblical and reformational emphasis on vocation as God's call must now be juxtaposed with a 1977 survey[10] conducted among two thousand clergy and laypersons in the Lutheran Church in America who were asked: "When you think of the word 'vocation,' which of the following comes to your mind most readily?"

	Clergy	Laypersons
God wants us to live a responsible Christian life in whatever we do	68%	11%
God calls one to enter some specific occupation as doctor or teacher	13%	14%
An occupation	14%	65%
Ordained ministry		1%
Full-time Christian work		1%
The word is unfamiliar		3%

Instead of the term "vocation" being elevated to describe only religious orders as in the Middle Ages, we are faced today with the opposite situation: the word has frequently been reduced to a secular dimension only. Many laypersons tend to equate vocation almost exclusively with an occupation.

So what should be done? Forsake the term "vocation"? Elevate it, so that life and particularly one's work take on a kind of halo of meaning?

I would suggest that we need to stop equating our calling only with what we do for a living. We are called to be followers of Jesus Christ not simply in what we *do* for a living, but in all that we *are*. Vocation involves our relationships with others, with nature, with the world, all seen within the primary call of God in our lives. The chief end of humankind is to glorify God, which is not a task but a gracious way of being. We *are* more than we do. We are called to be "in Christ," to live in the light of his cross. That calling is valid whether we have a meaningful job, a boring job, or no job at all. Vocation involves the whole sweep of life; the call of Christ claims all that we are.

Vocation is too often regarded as an absolute, a frozen something, a demand that can be fully defined. Instead of such an abstract and fixed notion of vocation, our calling is dynamic and continuous. It is a process involving search, self-criticism, learning, and faith in God.

Thus vocation is not a limited demand which can be satisfied by a decision to work in a particular sphere. Instead, vocation is to be used as God wills. We receive our vocation, or more precisely, we "uncover" it. Our vocation is not presented to us all nicely wrapped in aluminum foil and tied with a pretty ribbon. Our calling comes through life experiences in our skills, interests, and opportunities which God bestows on us. Vocation is the realization that God has intentionally given to each of us the combination of talents, abilities, and responsibilities which only each of us has.

God seeks us and finds and calls us where we are. Our response to the call of God, no matter what our particular setting or occupation, is to be the presence of Christ to those around us. Our vocation is the call to give ourselves in the ministry of the whole people of God for the life of the world.

NOTES

1. *Lumen Gentium,* chap. IV, sec. 31.

2. *Baptism, Eucharist and Ministry* (Geneva: World Council of Churches, 1982), 20.

3. *The New Delhi Report* (New York: World Council of Churches, 1962), 88.

4. Herman G. Stuempfle, Jr., *Theological and Biblical Perspectives on the Laity* (New York: Division for Mission in North America, Lutheran Church in America, 1973), 3.

5. Ibid., 4.

6. Cited in Paul Althaus, *The Theology of Martin Luther,* translated by Robert C. Schultz (Philadelphia: Fortress Press, 1966), 314.

7. Robert L. Calhoun, "Work and Vocation in Christian History," in *Work and Vocation,* edited by John Oliver Nelson (New York: Harper & Brothers, 1954), 82–115.

8. Ibid., 103.

9. "Church Postils," in *The Precious and Sacred Writings of Martin Luther,* edited by J. N. Lenker (Minneapolis: Lutherans of All Lands Co., 1950), 242–43.

10. "Lutheran Listening Post Survey Number Three," Office for Research and Planning, Lutheran Church in America.

4

Being Gifted

As CHRISTIANS in ministry, we would begin not with what we do for Christ but with what God has given us. God has given us everything: the gift of life itself, the gift of grace and salvation made tangible in our baptism, the gifts of healthy bodies and minds for most of us, and the gift of the Spirit to be present in all arenas of our lives.

Every moment and every place is a gift of the Creator, and each of us is unique in our particular combination of circumstances.

Paul wrote to the church at Corinth, "In each of us the Spirit is manifested in one particular way, for some useful purpose" (1 Cor. 12:7, NEB). The ways in which the Spirit manifests himself in our lives are what we call *gifts*. Our gifts are those qualities which God calls forth to be used to serve needs around us. The ministry of the *laos* (the people of God) is the use of our gifts to strengthen and support others for the sake of Christ. The apostle Peter clearly expresses the relationship of gifts and ministry: "As each has received a gift, employ it for one another, as good stewards of God's varied grace" (1 Pet. 4:10). Note that the writer insists that each has received a gift, that such gifts are varied, and that the gifts are to be used for others.

It is important for us, therefore, to be aware of our gifts from God and then to use our gifts freely in the ministries of our lives.

Recognizing Gifts

There is a story about Michelangelo that pictures him pushing a large rock down a street. A curious neighbor asked him: "Why do you work so hard over an old piece of stone?" Michelangelo answered: "Because there is an angel in that rock that wants to come out."

When I think about gifts, I think of that story. Each of us has the task and responsibility to recognize our God-given gifts.

God's gifts are so varied that there is no need to exclude and no need to convert. And such gifts should not be limited to talents. Rather, the gifts of God include

—our person (who we are)

—our specific situation

—our particular characteristics

By beginning in this way the emphasis is not first of all on what each does or can do, but simply on who we are and where we are.

This *givenness* is a gift and should be recognized as such. Rather than attempting to be something they are not, Christians are simply what they are. Their givenness is used for what God intended them to be. God calls us forth, not first of all as persons of skills, but as persons.

The application form for the Peace Corps for some time had a very perceptive question: How would you react to having the applicant as a guest in your home for six months? Such a question has obviously little to do with one's skills or one's academic ability, but rather emphasizes the total person, the givenness.

God calls us in our totality. The Spirit works within our entire beings and in our surroundings to cultivate the gifts of grace in our lives.

Our gifts are recognized as we do, not discovered before we do. More and more I am convinced that Paul's experience was the exception rather than the rule in the process of gift discovery. That is, he knew his ministry in advance (see Acts 22:14–15). He knew that he was to be the missionary to the Gentiles before he ever started. For most of us, however, that discovery is made known *as we do.* Thus, our ministries are discovered as we avail ourselves to obvious tasks around us. It is therefore more accurate to speak of recognizing our gifts than of discovering them.

As we seek to discover or recognize our ministry, there are certain clues available to us:

What do you see? Many miss their ministries by waiting for some mystical call, while all around them there is work to be done. It is a good rule that if no call seems obvious, then do the obvious. It may be that the discovery will take place in the act of doing. Is there a young people's group in need of a leader? A nursing home in need of volunteers? What do you see?

What do you enjoy? What is it that you thoroughly enjoy doing that gives you immense pleasure and satisfaction? A friend enjoyed archery and eventually became the chaplain for a statewide archer's organization. What do you enjoy? This may be a clue simply because it fits you.

What do you feel? What burdens you? What hurts you when you see it? What renders up an ache when you encounter it? What voids do you wish to see filled? A Christian who had gone through the trauma of a divorce started a ministry group for divorcees simply because she knew the hurt and the need. What burdens you? Children without parents? The ghetto? Alcoholics? That burden may be a clue.

What do you hear? Finally, as you seek your ministry, what do you hear others say about your gifts? Is there confirmation of your gifts from those who are close and honest? Do others affirm you? Do those whom you seek to serve seem helped? What do you hear?

None of these clues alone or all together are proof positive. But they are a part of the evidence. Look seriously. You are gifted—for ministry, a ministry in daily work and life.

An Abundance of Gifts

The Spirit is at work through and in an abundance of spiritual gifts. A biblical list illustrates the variety of gifts:

the gift of wisdom and knowledge (1 Cor. 12:8)
the gift of faith (1 Cor. 12:9)
the gift of healing (1 Cor. 12:9)
the gift of teaching (Rom. 12:7; 1 Cor. 12:28; 14:26)
the gift of exhortation or consolation (Rom. 12:8)
the gift of service (Rom. 12:7; 1 Pet. 4:11)
the gift of speaking (1 Pet. 4:11)
the gift of discerning spirits (1 Cor. 12:10)
the gift of administering (1 Cor. 12:28)

The various spiritual gifts bestowed among Christians reflect those given to the disciples and to the priests in biblical times as well as to the disciple and priest today:

the gift of listening
the gift of patience

the gift of caring
the gift of anger over injustice
the gift of personal witnessing
the gift of praying, either aloud with others or in private intercessory prayer
the gift of stirring things up
Still another way of discerning our gifts is to speak of special talents
which may become part of a ministry in Christ:
the gift of analyzing and problem solving
the gift of a good sense of humor
the gift of a smiling face
the gift of seriousness
the gift of enthusiasm
the gift of sensitivity
the gift of conversation
the gift of mediating broken relationships
the gift of counseling
the gift of perseverance
the gift of producing
the gift of intelligence
the gift of athletic prowess
the gift of musical ability
the gift of cooking or baking
the gift of sewing
the gift of nurture to plants or animals
the gift of writing
the gift of painting or sculpting
the gift of imagination
Perhaps you are able to identify gifts on these lists which you have
already been employing in ministry. Perhaps you recognize a gift that
you or a member of your family or a friend possesses, but that you did
not perceive as a God-given characteristic helpful to ministry. Someone may say, for example: "Nancy, you are a good listener. I can tell
that you really heard what I was saying!" Or: "John, I appreciate the
way you act as a father to your children. It gives me ideas about being a
father." Or: "You really seem to know how to solve problems in our
committee, Alice. I'm glad you're here." Such statements of affirmation that identify gifts may be quite surprising to these people. None of

them may realize that they have such characteristics or that these gifts are a part of ministry. When they actually hear such words, the gifts are recognized. We are invited to see ourselves and each other as gift-bearing and gift-evoking persons.

When Jesus saw Levi, the tax collector, he saw a Matthew in him that needed uncovering. To see one another in such a way is not, first of all, to point out what is good or to engage in backslapping or phony positive thinking. Rather, it is to see gifts of God that can be celebrated, received in joy, and developed in ministry.

To evoke gifts from within others is one of the greatest opportunities for ministry. W. O. Thomason calls these people who are enabled to do this for each other "life givers."

> We can thank God that always among us are people, life givers, who have the capacity to see within us what we are and what we can be. How often has anyone talked for a moment, then minutes, or an hour about what you might become? Most of us can count on one hand the times in our life when this has happened. The life giver is one who has the capacity to see possibilities in persons when all others around see impossibilities.[1]

Exercising Gifts for Ministry

All of these gifts are not distributed equally, either in number or in quality. Actually, we all have many gifts, but circumstances cause us to develop only certain ones. The others go unnoticed or have to be kept latent while we use the ones that are the most appropriate. And one gift is no greater or lesser than another. The Scriptures clearly teach that each person has at least one gift, and further, Scripture promises the same reward to all—the joy of exercising that gift.

The well-known parable of the three servants, which Jesus told to his disciples, points out to us the use of one's gifts (Matt. 25:14-30). One servant was given five bags of money, another two, and another one, "each according to his ability" (Matt. 25:15). The servant with five bags put the money to use and doubled his investment. So did the servant with two bags. The last servant, however, buried his bag within the ground because of his fear of risking what he had.

Note that the first two servants, although their number of talents was not identical, nevertheless received promotions: "Well done, good and faithful servant; you have been faithful over a little, I will set you over much; enter into the joy of your master" (Matt. 25:21).

We may overlook our gifts because we think we are supposed to be humble. ("I just don't see any gifts on those lists which apply to me." "What if my attempt to witness to a fellow employee ends in a disaster?" "What if others do not approve?") We are not asked to succeed; we are only asked to invest what we have and to leave the outcome to God. We do not have to be better than others or live up to their expectations or fulfill their demands. We need only be faithful to the Spirit of God, who is present in our lives.

Sometimes each of us recognizes and develops gifts that others wanted us to develop. We have nurtured these gifts to please them or to get ahead. In the process, though, we may have buried gifts that were not as valued by others. In our ministry we are free to use the gifts that seem most significant to us. As God calls them forth in ministry, they are expanded often beyond our imagining. They may be the gifts that have been buried deep within us, never used, in a part of us we have always hidden. In the Lord's parable he invited us to risk these gifts for ministry.

Just as by losing one's life, one finds it, so by risking one's gifts, they are secured. We are responsible for investing our gifts, for spending them in the world. That is one reason why the kingdom of God is likened to salt, seed, leaven, and light. It is a starter. The gift grows when it is planted and glows when it is lighted.

Our gifts are complemented by the gifts given other members in the church. The community of Christians called the church is a body, the body of Christ, and each diverse part has a function. Thus a community of Christians is a collection of gifts, a kaleidoscopic variety which brings out each person's strengths and carries each person's weaknesses. Out of the Spirit's infinite imagination come the variety of the gifts that the community of Christ possesses. The apostle Paul's imagery of the church as a body with many members as well as his celebration of the rich abundance of gifts portrayed in 1 Corinthians 12 points to the fact that the gifts are so varied that there is no need to exclude. Gifts are therefore the ways in which the Spirit manifests himself in our lives. The ministry of the people of God is the use of our gifts to strengthen and support others for the sake of Christ.

A vital church identifies, affirms, encourages, and exercises the gifts that the Spirit has given the members of the body. Such an evoking of gifts has nothing to do with cheap flattery or self-aggrandizement or pride. By beginning with who each one is, stewardship becomes the evocation, care, and exercise of the gifts we are given. The church is healthy when every cell, every person, is at work sharing his or her gifts to meet the needs of others. Out of such oneness of Spirit and such diversity of gifts, the work of Christ in the world is called forth.

When we look around at the gifts God has given others we may be provoked to envy or jealousy. Or we may use our gifts out of pride or with selfish motives. But if the gifts are used for the one body, the one Spirit, the one faith, they combine into a mighty force.

Someone once asked Rembrandt at what point a painting was complete. To this the famed Dutch artist replied, "A painting is finished when it expresses the intent of the artist." So it is with our lives. They are complete when we express the full intent of Christ, when we are his gifts of service in each moment of our daily lives.

NOTES

1. W. O. Thomason, *The Life Givers* (Nashville: Broadman Press, 1972), 56–57.

PART TWO

ARENAS OF MINISTRY

5

Family

WHEN MY COUSIN Jim was preparing to leave for college, everyone in his family was excited about the event and wanted to be helpful. His sister Karen, age six, enthusiastically volunteered to polish his shoes. Jim, although a bit dubious, agreed. The next morning he found his shoes neatly placed next to his bed. Not only were the sides all shined but also the heels, and even the soles were completely covered with polish. It was a sign to Jim that his kid sister really loved him, even if she didn't know how to shine shoes.

Family life is an arena in which God's grace and goodness are revealed. God's love is reflected in the human caring which makes family relationships constructive.

I do not mean to paint only a rosy or sentimental picture of what family life actually is. Separation, divorce, and death break up families. Tensions, such as may be caused by three generations living together in a family unit or children breaking away and rebelling, frequently make the strains almost unbearable. Husbands and wives and children sometimes turn on one another in hate and jealousy. We are hurt more often and more deeply in our families than we are in any other relationships.

Yet it is nothing less than amazing that two and three or even seven or eight different individuals can and do live together in the same space. Each of us knows that within our families, most of the time, we are accepted for who we are, not for what we ought to be or for what others want us to be. We know that homes are places where love can be central. The home is the point in our culture at which there is more of a chance than anywhere else to demonstrate the plan of God's creation in action.

All of us—single, married, separated, divorced, widowed—are members of a family. Our families include not only the immediate members who live in the same house as we—our living unit—but also the brothers and sisters already out of the house, the grandparents, and the entire network of those who are related to one another. A family is a set of functions and relationships. In these relationships each of us finds a need and a desire to minister and to be ministered to. This life together in families is a model of all of our life in the community and the world. Ministry is taught and learned in the family. The question, therefore, is: How do we minister to one another in our families?

The Ministry of Caring

We minister by providing the three basic needs of food, clothing, and shelter for one another and for those in our families who cannot provide for themselves. Infants, the elderly, and the sick all must have their needs fulfilled, preferably by the immediate family, and if that is not possible, then by the larger human family called society. The father, the mother, and the children by their labor provide many of these basic needs as they prepare the meals and do the dishes and the rest of the household duties. They form a network of caring for one another.

Such a network is not automatic. The basic needs of warm clothing, good food, and shelter are not to be taken for granted. Many people, both in this country and throughout the world, go to sleep warm and well-fed because they have a family and their family has an income. Others have neither. If we have access to more of the world's goods than we need, we can extend our caring.

We also minister by giving love. All of us are aware that a family provides more than material care. It ministers to the wholeness of persons. An atmosphere of love is a ministry.

Which is more important, spending time with the family or spending it on improving our occupations so the family will be assured of the necessities and have more opportunities? That is a great tension in many lives. So many jobs consume extra hours. Maybe you run a store or have to hold two jobs, or you are a trucker, or you have the chance of being a manager if you carry work home and move your family every other year. If so, you know the tension.

Or maybe your children are grown and maybe their lives are not going as you had hoped, and you are wondering whether you gave them enough of yourself and your time when they were young, or whether you gave them too much. The tension can hurt. But it is a sign of conscientious ministry. We want to be good ministers and serve our families well. The tension is necessary to keep us trying for the best balance of ministry.

If there is a choice, I guess I would advise that we choose family time rather than occupation time. We have a bigger stake in the family than in our employment. We can try to change business associates, if we need to, and we can leave a good job for a poor one if need be, but we cannot change children. If we lose the struggle in our occupational interests, we can try again; but if we neglect our children or parents, our loss cannot be corrected.

Family time is also more than loving time. It is a time for communicating, setting goals and values, making decisions, establishing traditions, having fun, and developing spiritual awareness.

We are tied to one another in our family relationships. As a friend of mine has said, in families we learn what it means to stick with and be stuck with. That is the givenness of family; we are placed in a family without choice. Thus the relationships are unconditional; they simply cannot be set aside. That tie provides bonds of cooperation and support, but bonds may also become a bondage. Dictatorial parenting, childhood selfishness, and overprotective grandparenting may become chains which put a drag on the caring process. Rather than encouraging a mutual ministry, such situations can increase the tension already present. But caring love claims the other person in the face of all that is unlovable and unattractive. Most members of families do care for one another, no matter what. God has designed it that way and that is their ministry.

We received an amusing mimeographed Christmas letter last year. It came from a family that had three children in college and one at home. The letter listed the successes of the children in college and the activities of Mom and Dad, but left out the child at home. Then in a handwritten ''P.S.,'' the life of the fourth child was described. You could see what had happened. They had gotten so preoccupied with

the promising careers of the three at college that they had forgotten
the one at home. The news of the family was mimeographed on the
back of their Christmas card; when the family discovered they had
inadvertently left out the fourth child, they did not have time to do a
new card and had to hand-scribe the "P.S." It was one of those little
kinds of mistakes we make once in a while. I wish more Christmas
letters would evidence more failures. It would be a ministry to me
knowing that I am not the only one who is not perfect.

The family is a place to share failures as well as successes. We bear
one another's burdens in the family. That goes for the distant relatives
with whom we exchange greetings as well as for those living in the
same household. We can have an atmosphere of honesty in which no
one is afraid of anyone else. The family lives at a deeper level. It is the
caring center—a place to be gentle and to touch, a place to be cuddled
and tickled, to be counseled and affirmed.

There are so many ministries a family performs. Each member
cares for the others in such concrete ways as having little inside jokes
that only other members of the family know about, making time for
listening, doing fun things together, and praying together.

The Ministry of Growing

When I was in high school, I had to come down the stairs sideways
in the morning because the arches in my feet hurt so badly. The doctor
called it growing pains. Families have growing pains, too, because all
the members of the family are growing. Not only is physical growth
taking place but spiritual and psychological growth as well. Just when
parents have learned what it means to have a teenager in the house,
that individual has become a young adult. A family normally encourages each member to be his or her own person while at the same time
acknowledging common traits.

Change sometimes frightens us, but growth is change. We are
human *becomings* more than we are human *beings*. We learn from
each other's growth and change. Our individual differences may become the very ways by which God gets through to us. When God has
work to do, he most often does it through people. God teaches toler-
ance and compassion, tenderness and justice, integrity and love,
through those who are closest to us—the members of our families.

The ministry of growth takes place within our families because the family unit is a testing ground. The family is the basic place where one learns the meaning of yes and no. Adolescents particularly are testing who they are and what they can and will become. No other unit in our society does as much stretching and pulling and pushing as the family. How far can I go? What does my individuality mean? How free and responsible am I to be? In answering each question within the day-to-day living in a family, all members are experiencing a ministry which, through word and example, demonstrates the love and obedience which flows from God in our lives.

Inevitably, conflict arises within families. In the first family in the Bible the rivalry was so great that one member of the family murdered his brother (Gen. 4:1–16). The Cain and Abel story is but a prelude to later family conflicts: the bitter Jacob and Esau relationship, with mother Rebekah favoring Jacob, the narrative of Joseph and the jealousy of his brothers, and the tragic story of David and his rebellious son Absalom. The Scriptures also report family conflicts centering on drunkenness (Noah), adultery (David; Hosea), lying (Samson), jealousy (between the elder brother and the prodigal son), misunderstanding of roles (Mary and Martha), and many more. God's people were far from perfect. But God continued to work in and through these persons. Frequently, out of these family conflicts came the strength of faith in God. New understandings of God resulted from the struggles within the family.

A friend of mine told me that his family sometimes plays a game around the table at their house. Each person describes the next member of the family in terms of a flower, a piece of fruit, a piece of furniture, or an article of clothing. My friend says it is fun but scary, because both humorous and hurtful things come out. I would add that the members of his family in that game are ministering to one another.

We minister not only by accepting each other's changes and encouraging them but also by growing ourselves and letting others share in the accomplishment. Much of a family's growth is a ministry.

6

Occupation

WHAT OCCUPIES our time—that is one of the main arenas of our ministry. For some, occupation is a paid job; for others, it is being a student or being retired. For still others, it is homemaking and volunteer activities. For the unemployed, the main occupation may be seeking a job. But for all, a crucial question is: How do we spend the major part of our time? That is our occupation.

What we have in common in our occupations is some form of work: working to fix roofs, working at an algebra problem, working to get a job, working to make meals, working at our hobbies. All life must be worked at: protected, planted, replanted, fashioned, cooked for, coaxed, diapered, farmed, sustained. Work is the way we tend the world, the way people connect.

A series of questions interspersed with personal vignettes will give us a perspective to see how ministry and occupation are related.

Meaning

What kind of day do you have most Mondays? Does your occupation have meaning?

Carl Murray Bates, age fifty-seven, a stonemason since the age of seventeen, is quoted in Studs Terkel's book *Working:*

I can't imagine a job where you go home and maybe go by a year later and you don't know what you've done. My work, I can see what I did the first day I started. All my work is set right out there in the open and I can look at it as I go by. It's something I can see the rest of my life. Forty years ago, the first blocks I ever laid in my life, when I was seventeen years old. I never go through Eureka—a litle town down there on the river—that I don't look thataway. It's always there.

   Immortality as far as we're concerned. Nothin' in this world lasts forever, but did you know that stone—Bedford limestone, they claim—deteriorates one-sixteenth of an inch every hundred years? And it's around four or five inches for a house. So that's gettin' awful close. (Laughs.)[1]

Do you put your work too high? Too low? A mother who is determined to have a *Better Homes and Gardens* house and spends about ten minutes a day with her child has made a decision about meaning. An employee who says, "I am just a filing clerk," or someone who says, "I am only a kindergarten teacher," has also made a judgment about the meaning of occupation.

Work is a search for enduring meaning as well as for daily bread, for recognition as well as for pay, for service to others as well as for one's own self-worth and pride. Most of all, work is a search for growth rather than stagnation, for life rather than death.

Just because we see our work as ministry does not mean that the work itself is different. There is no such thing as Christian farming. Farming may be done by Christians, but it is no more godly because it is. All farming is godly because God created all food production. God created all people. As they serve one another by their work, that work is of God whether the worker knows it or not. The Christian simply has the privilege of knowing it is of God. That knowledge gives meaning and purpose to the work.

Work can have more meaning as a ministry because in a way it can be something we truly give of ourselves. It is really the only thing we can give to God and to others that is our own. We do not produce our talents or the natural resources with which we work, but we do produce our toil. Our energy and thought have gone into the work, whether the result is a bench made by a carpenter, a class taught by a teacher, a floor mopped by a homemaker, or a package delivered by a truck driver. In that sense, we can say with the psalmist:

   Let the favor of the Lord our God be upon us, and establish thou the work of our hands upon us, yea, the work of our hands establish thou it. (Ps. 90:17)

To establish oneself is to gain recognition, to be accepted, to make firm. That recognition is desperately needed by many. Some jobs are meaningless no matter how we view them. They may be jobs created just to make work, or jobs created by a system that doesn't know how useless the work is, or jobs that are so toilsome they cause more suffering than they relieve.

What has a man from all the toil and strain with which he toils beneath the sun? For all his days are full of pain, and his work is a vexation; even in the night his mind does not rest. (Eccles. 2:22–23)

We cannot gloss over these realities just by calling them ministries. We can only say God notices. He recognizes the pain and indignity, and he hurts with the victims who are trapped in these jobs.

Choice

Do you choose to do what you do on Monday mornings?

All people hunger for a sense of calling, that is, a feeling that their particular work needs to be done, and that it needs them to do it. That is what the word "vocation" means—a sense of calling. Actually the word has two meanings. In the biblical sense it means that each is called by God himself to the tasks of life. In the secular sense vocation means a purposeful occupation and the skills that go with it. For example, one learns the occupation of mechanic by going to a vocational school. One's sense of vocation thus may include both the call of God and the call of craft.

Those who do have a choice need to think a bit about why they have made the choice they have. We picked up a hitchhiker once who was on his way to a nursing home where he worked as an orderly. "There must be a lot of satisfaction taking care of the people there," we surmised. "I'm not in it for that," he quickly responded. "I'm in it for the pay."

He knew the reason for his choice and he was honest about it. The reason wasn't altogether dishonorable. A lot of difficult jobs wouldn't get done if it weren't for the compensation. He had needs, the elderly had needs, and they were getting together. That is the way a job works in many cases. But the orderly may have been missing out on other good reasons for choosing that occupation. Maybe he could endure the incontinent ward a little longer than others. That is a calling one could be proud of. Paul tells his Ephesian friends to "live a life that measures up to the standard God set when he called you" (Eph. 4:1,

TEV). The standard that Jesus set was touching the lepers when everyone considered it too horrible to do so. The orderly could have sensed this higher calling in his work and kept the money besides.

Choosing doesn't always mean changing; it means being aware of the reasons for doing what we are doing. Becoming aware of the reasons for our choices helps us become aware of the ministries we are performing.

Quality

Do you have any control over the quality of what you will do this Monday?

Quality work is a ministry. It is a way of serving the employer or the consumer, and oneself as well. It is good for self-worth.

Hub Dillard, a crane operator, also speaking in Terkel's book *Working*, described the feeling:

> There's a certain amount of pride—I don't care how *little* you did. You drive down the road and you say, "I worked on this road." If there's a bridge, you say, "I worked on this bridge." Or you drive by a building and you say, "I worked on this building." Maybe it don't mean anything to anybody else, but there's a certain pride knowing you did your bit.
>
> That building we put up, a medical building. Well, that granite was imported from Canada. It was really expensive. Well, I set all this granite around there. So you do this and you don't make a scratch on it. It's food for your soul that you know you did it good. Where somebody walks by this building you can say, "Well, I did that."[2]

It has been said that God does not so much need people to do extraordinary things as he needs ordinary people who do ordinary things extraordinarily well. Ministering has more to do with how we do a job than with what we do.

At the end of Terkel's talk with Mr. Bates, Bates says:

> There's not a house in this country that I haven't built that I don't look at every time I go by. (Laughs.) I can set here now and actually in my mind see so many that you wouldn't believe. If there's one stone in there crooked, I know where it's at and I'll never forget it. Maybe thirty years, I'll know a place where I should have took that stone out and redone it but I didn't. I still notice it. The people who live there might not notice it, but I notice it. I never pass that house that I don't think of it. I've got one house in mind right now. (Laughs.) That's the work of my hands. 'Cause you see, stone, you don't prepaint it, you don't camouflage it. It's there, just like I left it forty years ago.[3]

All of life is a part of the creation God loves. In Christ, God has put a new value on everything. He works out the meaning of this new relationship in his call to us. This calling is all-encompassing: "And whatever you do, in word or deed, do everything in the name of the Lord Jesus, giving thanks to God the Father through him" (Col. 3:17). We belong wholly to Jesus Christ. He is the one who calls us. His calling comes to us in everything we do. Quality is the name of ministry.

Growth

This Monday will you be doing something a bit differently and a bit better than the way you did it last Monday? Does your occupation allow growth?

Growth is another evidence of ministry. The mental, spiritual, and physical growth that takes place in one's work affects one's attitudes and services. Strangely enough, this growth can take place in more ways than one realizes.

An auto worker, speaking in J. Oliver Nelson's *Work and Vocation,* observes the effects of working on an assembly line:

> For the first day or the first week or month, incredible as it sounds, your job will be quite interesting. An assembly line is, after all, a remarkable thing. At first you'll be curious not only about your own job, but the jobs of others and even operations in other parts of the plant. This will wear off. In a few months you'll find other things to think about, or I should say, dream about, for by now you can do your operation blind-folded, leaving your mind to wander where it will. Then after a year or so, you'll find another strange thing happening to you. You'll find that your mind has little or nothing to think or dream about. At this point, you'll begin to know for the first time what it's "really" like to work in a shop.
>
> During your dreamy stage, maybe you'll bring a book to work to read during your lunch hour or relief. But you'll run into a snag here too. You'll find yourself dreaming while you read. Other barriers to concentration will be clock-watching and the terrific noise of hammers and machine and the distraction of the conversations along side of you. This inability to concentrate will carry over into your after-office hours, too, and it will take considerable prodding on your part and the part of your friends to keep yourself mentally alert. . . . At this point you will understand, perhaps, why sensationalist literature has such an appeal for workers. At the end of the day, you'll realize also why movies, particularly the light, happy-ending, refreshing ones enjoy such popularity.[4]

This worker went through four stages: (1) curiosity, (2) dreaming,

(3) nothing to dream about, and (4) inability to concentrate. Growth? On first thought no, but in a way yes. The mind is a fantastic creation. It has a way of adjusting when a job is unbearably monotonous. The mind can even shut down and turn itself off to keep its person from going mad with boredom. We have to recognize that adjustment as one kind of growth. It is necessary so that the people on assembly lines can bear to serve us. We have to find a better way to produce goods, but until we do we can be grateful to those who minister to us by enduring monotony. We have to affirm them for being able to grow enough to endure it.

The growth from boredom to stimulation, though, has another more satisfying ministry. A person who is alive and alert and curious finds satisfaction in work. And that is not related to the amount of education or intelligence, the salary of the job, or the prestige of the position. My barber and my service station operator, for example, reveal more of these characteristics than do some of my colleagues with doctoral degrees. To be interested in others or in the way things are put together or in ways to improve the performance of one's work—such attention is the best antidote for boredom and monotony. Every kind of work has its own tedium. Boredom essentially happens within. "I am bored" is more often said than "The job is boring."

Some will say that growth is more likely to be present with the worker who deals with persons than the worker who deals with things. But the meaning of the work is not lessened simply because one serves a remote neighbor. Many a life has been saved by a properly tightened screw.

Relationships with Others

How many persons will you be working with this Monday?

Ministry happens in our relationships with others. It is in our work, whether in the office, the home, the classroom, or the factory. These are the places where we are with neighbors, those whom God tells us we are to love and to serve. In our work we touch others and are touched by those around us.

How do we see those with whom we work? Do we see them merely as customers? Do we view students as persons or as team members? If we are employers, do we see each worker as a person in his or her own right? Or is each only a cog in an efficient machine?

This Monday, will you be working mostly with things or with

people? In the pressures and tensions of work, whether in the office or the home, we sometimes begin to treat others as things rather than as persons. When we see those around us as persons, images of the Creator, men and women who too have a purpose and vocation in life, we grow in our roles as ministers and priests who serve others for the sake of Jesus Christ.

Although verbal witness to others is always a mandate for Christians, the time and place for such witness must be appropriate. To quote Scripture and to offer to pray with a fellow worker may hurt the ministry of Christ if a credible relationship has not already been established.

Luther had a way of turning things into tools for serving people:

If you are a manual laborer, you find that the Bible has been put into your workshop, into your hand, into your heart. It teaches and preaches how you should treat your neighbor. Just look at your tools—at your needle or thimble, your beer barrel, your goods, your scales or yardstick or measure—and you will read this statement inscribed on them. Everywhere you look, it stares at you. Nothing that you handle every day is so tiny that it does not continually tell you this, if you will only listen. Indeed, there is no shortage of preaching. You have as many preachers as you have transactions, goods, tools, and other equipment in your house and home. All this is continually crying out to you: "Friend, use me in your relations with your neighbor just as you would want your neighbor to use his property in his relations with you."[5]

The things are "preachers." The "preaching" is in the way we use things to serve. The preaching is in the shoptalk and the transactions, in the nitty-gritty of the work each of us is in. Our care for others is shown in the way we greet them and talk with them during the coffee break and the lunch hour. Such conversation may seem unimportant, but it may be the foundation on which is built a relationship. When a crisis occurs in a person's life, he or she may turn to someone who has shown concern in the past. What was said or done yesterday carries over into today's relationship. It may be that no one will come up to you and want to discuss a problem, but as often as not someone will mention a problem in the course of a conversation just to get your feeling about it. We are often sought out informally without realizing it. Nor do we need always to be aware that we are counseling when we are, because there is a danger in thinking, Oh, now I am being asked for counsel, I must act like a counselor. The professionalism may be artificial and hurt the relationship. Our ministries are performed constantly in every caring relationship. When we listen to the problems of others we are aware of the anxiety, loneliness, and fears within each of us. We share joys and express disappointments and in that way recognize the human need of belonging to one another.

Challenge

This Monday morning, at what points will your occupation challenge your Christian faith? At what points will it limit the challenge of your faith?

Greg, age thirty-six, an architect, comments:

> At work, what I see is so much conflict. The client want this, my company says that, and I'm in the middle of it. I work with school boards a lot on buildings. Sometimes I get so disgusted, because the last thing some of them seem interested in is education itself. I do the best job I can, but I have to grit my teeth sometimes.
>
> Like yesterday, I got a call from a contractor. He wanted to know why we had changed some specifications. ''Lack of funds,'' I replied. Even he knew we were cheating on the quality of the job. I had fought that change. If I hadn't fought it, a lot more specs would have been changed. I get phone calls like that often. Sometimes I think it is God calling, just to keep me honest.
>
> The last two years have opened my eyes to a lot of things. It's scary, but exciting. Funny thing, in all this hassle, God actually seems closer to me. Where all this is going, I really don't know.

We don't even have to look for challenges. They are there most of the time, in a phone call, on the accounts, in the office gossip, in a mechanical problem in the company report, in a sinkful of dishes, or in the foreman we can't stomach. These are the intersections between faith and work.

A crucial question is: How does my occupation contribute to what God wants done in the world? The world is an intricate network of dependence and accountability. God's creation uses the activities of human beings as part of the ordering of the world and the nurturing of the earth. Our occupations may become the partnership of co-creation with God, of being God's hands of work and God's arms of care in the world.

The challenge is to be Christlike—to care and to risk. Sometimes we hesitate to stand up for the right because we do not feel we are good enough ourselves. We are afraid others will say, "Look who's talking." But as Christians we don't claim to be 100 percent perfect, not even 50 percent perfect. We claim only to be human beings, sinners saved by the grace of God. Sometimes we make a mess of things and lose our temper, or make fools of ourselves. But we struggle with God's help, from day to day. That is our commitment to Christ. Out of the tensions of the actual encounter between our Christian faith and the world of work come the kinds of ministries that do meet the demands of the gospel and the realities of our concrete world.

NOTES

1. Studs Terkel, *Working: People Talk About What They Do All Day and How They Feel About What They Do* (New York: Pantheon Books, 1974), 22.

2. Ibid., 54.

3. Ibid., 21–22.

4. John Oliver Nelson, ed., *Work and Vocation* (New York: Harper & Brothers, 1954), 157.

5. *Luther's Works,* vol. 21, edited by Jaroslav Pelikan (St. Louis: Concordia Publishing House, 1956), 237.

7

Work

THE GREEKS looked down on physical work. The Bible writers looked up to it. They viewed it as part of the divine order of the world.

When God started creating the universe, he certainly was working, the Scriptures tell us, and enjoying it. The first work done in the creation was done by God himself, culminating in the sculpture of his own image—humanity. And all of this work was a weekday kind of work.

Work Created by God

Someone has called the Bible a book by workers, about workers, for workers. You do get that feeling from the creation stories. Adam was placed on earth "to till it and keep it" (Gen. 2:15).

Adam and Eve were to do the work of raising a family—"be fruitful and multiply"—and they were to do the work of keeping the irrigation ditches in operation, which was what the desert peoples meant when they said they were to "subdue" the earth (Gen. 1:28).

Our first glimpse of human beings, then, was as parents and as farmers cultivating and developing the ground. God probably could have put a palace in paradise, complete with television and electric lights, with a limousine at the gate of the garden and an Eden expressway on which to ride. But the all-wise Creator must have wanted his creatures to have the pleasure and the satisfaction of working at all of this. Eden was not a garden of the gods; it was a place for human beings, a place to reflect the image of God by being active in his service. Work is part of the divinely ordered structure of God's world.

But not everyone can whistle at work. Sinful conditions have turned many pleasures of work into pains. This is described in the story of the Fall:

And to Adam he said, "Because you have listened to the voice of your wife, and have eaten of the tree of which I commanded you, 'You shall not eat of it,' cursed is the ground because of you; in toil you shall eat of it all the days of your life; thorns and thistles it shall bring forth to you; and you shall eat the plants of the field. In the sweat of your face you shall eat bread till you return to the ground, for out of it you were taken; you are dust, and to dust you shall return." (Gen. 3:17–19)

Toil and sweat, thorns and thistles, death and dying make work burdensome and agonizing. We think of the work as a curse, but the curse of sin is not the work itself, but rather the drudgery which has been interjected into it by our sin. The presence of sin alters the conditions of work; what was formerly a matter of joyful service now becomes slavery and bondage. Children hate to go to school, homemakers shake their head over Monday morning mounds of laundry, and workers sometimes refer to their place of employment as the salt mine. Yet work is one of the major arenas in which we serve God and one another.

The Hebrews were concerned that everyone have fair reward and motivation for work. They wanted each person to have ownership— "They shall sit every man under his vine and under his fig tree" (Mic. 4:4). The Hebrews remembered the drudgery of work under slavery and passed laws that would give each person an opportunity to have the reward of ownership (Lev. 25:25–28). We can't each own land, but we can be aware of the factors that motivate work and develop them. That encourages the ministry of work.

Co-Workers with God

Scriptures make clear that God continues to work in nature and history and that our responsibility is to join in that work. Work must have integrity, because it affects the creation. When people build an arrogant tower or grow rich in houses and land but disregard the Word of the Lord, they court disaster (Gen. 11:1–9; Isa. 5:8–12). When the skill of the craftsperson is turned to the making of idols, it deserves ridicule (Isa. 44:9–20). But when the broken walls of Jerusalem are restored by faithful returning exiles, their leader can say: "This work had been accomplished with the help of our God" (Neh. 6:16).

God's work touches the work of human beings at many points. He gives to the crafts their artistry and cunning (Exod. 35:30–35). If the action achieves success, the worker cannot say that it is due solely to skill, wisdom, or power (Deut. 8:17–18). God brings "forth food from the earth" (Ps. 104:14). All natural and human resources are from God, not simply in terms of some distinct work of creation but also in terms of his continuous work of sustenance and purposeful guidance.

Failure. That is an element of our work sometimes too. What about the worker who moves from job to job, sometimes tired, sometimes fired? Relatives have names for him and family get fed up with him. Nothing seems to work out just right.

What about the failure of the employee who works conscientiously all his life but then one day opens the wrong valve or loses control for a moment and is laid off?

Is there ministry in failure? There is. The ministry is in knowing the grace of God. With God we are all both saints and failures at the same time. He makes us saints because he forgives our failures. Sometimes we must be laid off because God's justice requires accountability, but God's love is another matter. His grace never lays us off or remembers our failure. Every day is a new day in God's grace.

Achievement comes from God's grace, too. We do not produce the natural resources with which we work. They are gifts. Neither do we produce our motivation. It is mostly a result of the circumstances in which we live. We are aware of that when we are ill. One minute we can be highly motivated and the next minute we are flat on our backs unable to will ourselves to do a thing.

The Bible writers emphasized the person more than the position, the agent more than the act, the motive more than the mode. Ps. 127:1 says it well: "Unless the Lord builds the house, those who build it labor in vain. Unless the Lord watches over the city, the watchman stays awake in vain."

The psalmist does not place the work of masonry higher than army life, or vice versa. Instead, he addresses each worker to face the central question: Why and in what spirit is the work done? For the carpenter, the test is whether in building the house his energies are properly related to God's purpose.

The Ministry of Work: In and Through the Ordinary

The revelation of Jesus Christ came not in the form of a person of privilege nor of financial comfort. Jesus Christ found his friends among tax gatherers, fisherfolk, women of the streets, and simple householders as well as among people of wealth and position. His talk is full of illustrations from the work of vinedressers, woodworkers, shepherds, stewards, magistrates, and harvest hands. His parables referred to sowers (Matt. 13:3), home-building (Matt. 7:24), swine-tending (Luke 15:11), and housecleaning (Luke 15:8). In the life of Jesus Christ, there is no hint of alienation from everyday living and daily toil. His life was a life of service, witness, and prayer—the day-to-day process. The perfect vocation becomes clear in Jesus Christ, in whom both the divine calling and the human response meet. Jesus Christ revealed his mission in and through the ordinary.

The New Testament is filled with ordinary individuals whose lives were touched by Christ, and after that time, this relationship made all the difference. Their witness and variety of ministry in what we would call ordinary lives include:

fishermen	Peter, James and John
tax collectors	Matthew, Zacchaeus
the rich	Joseph of Arimathea
the lowly	Mary
shepherds	near Bethlehem
physician	Luke
dye worker	Lydia
carpenters	Joseph, Jesus Christ
homemaker	Martha
religious teacher	Nicodemus
tentmaker	Paul

Numerous others in the early Christian community, men and women, rich and poor, high and low, understood what it meant to be the salt of the earth, the light of the world, and the leaven within the loaf. They gave of themselves, as salt and light and leaven do, for the sake of the faith. They sensed what it meant to be a minister, a servant of Christ, and most of them either remained in the same occupation or returned to it after their Master ascended. Their service to Christ was in and through daily living. They continued to live out the Lord with their lives as the open book. It was no hit-and-run dropping of Care packages. They were ministers in who they were, and they lived and stayed where they were.

Carl Murray Bates, whom we quoted in the last chapter from *Working* by Studs Terkel, describes one of his days:

It's a pretty good day layin' stone or brick. Not tiring. Anything you like to do isn't tiresome. It's hard work; stone is heavy. At the same time, you get interested in what you're doing and you usually fight the clock the other way. You're not lookin' for quittin'. You're wondering you haven't got enough done and it's almost quittin' time. (Laughs.) I ask the hod carrier what time it is and he says two thirty. I say, "Oh, my Lord, I was gonna get a whole lot more than this."[1]

Being ordinary is not necessarily a virtue, but changing the world by ordinary service is. In the example of ordinary daily life, the Christian laypeople make their faith real to those around them. The arena of God's activity is not some abstract, ephemeral, spiritual world, but God is concretely present among those who confess his name. His Spirit moves and touches people where they are in the day-to-day round of life. To serve God and others in and through our work—that is the challenge that is always before us.

NOTES

1. Studs Terkel, *Working: People Talk About What They Do All Day and How They Feel About What They Do* (New York: Pantheon Books, 1974), 18.

8

Leisure

LEISURE AS an arena of ministry? You've got to be kidding!

Yet, if ministry is the total way our faith and living are related, then leisure is a place for giving and receiving ministry. But sometimes our attitudes about work and time get in the way of seeing leisure as an arena of ministry.

Leisure, Work, and Time

When the work ethic collides with the leisure life, guilt or pride results—guilt when the leisure time seemingly has to be justified ("I really needed this rest; I was worn out") or pride when the work seems so important the leisure has to be declined ("Why, I haven't taken a vacation in twenty years, not since my honeymoon").

The chief evidence of the conflict is that leisure is seen as the opposite of work. Work is taken as the evil that must be endured to make leisure possible, or leisure is taken as the evil that must be redeemed by work.

That is why this approach may seem contradictory, finding a ministry in leisure just after it found a ministry in work. But leisure and work are complementary. They form two purposeful parts of an integrated life. Saturday's ministries, as Mark Gibbs has called them, are also the arenas in which we are to be aware of our calling as Christians.

No doubt about it, we are becoming more time-conscious. Until the Middle Ages, the sun and sundials informed people of the time of day. By the twelfth century, bells were rung to indicate particular hours. Tower clocks came in the fourteenth century, and by 1550, pocket watches were rather common. Hands to mark seconds were added in 1590. And now we can wake up at night to see the time reflected on the bedroom ceiling.

Thus another problem seems to arise when leisure is equated with time. Sometimes this is revealed in the phrase "killing time." It implies that too much time can be a drag. Time of course can't be killed. At the end of the day or the end of life, time ends up the survivor. The time problem is revealed in the apology "I'm too busy," or the lament "They are too busy for us." Overloaded leisure time seems to deny fulfillment.

Some common expressions reveal the ambiguity about the relationship of time, leisure, and work.

—My work is absolutely boring—every day going back and doing the same thing for eight hours a day.

—Leisure? Ha! I'm busier than ever!

—Thirteen weeks off this year. What do I do with all that time? I'd rather go back to work.

—I've got all kinds of time on my hands since I retired at age fifty-eight.

—I have all these timesavers in my house, but I seem to have less free time than ever.

—Leisure revolution? What's that? I don't have time to think about it.

Leisure is a quality of life rather than a quantity of time. Leisure cannot be calculated by subtracting the time needed for work, sleep, and other necessities from the total hours in the day. That would indicate free time, but free time is not automatically leisure time. Free time is merely a framework in which leisure is possible. If free time were in itself the key to leisure, then the confined, the unemployed, and some of the retired would have too much and everyone else not enough.

Many unemployed and retired persons use their talents as refreshing gifts of ministry. But more than that, retirement especially can be a time when a person is valuable in his or her own right, quite apart from the job or even volunteer services. The ministry is in the being, a being made of God, baptized in Christ, free in the Spirit. Many retired persons witness just by the grace of their being, showing what a gift from God life really is.

Much ministry takes place during leisure time—ministry in families, in congregations, in communities. Laughing (at a good television comedy), being with friends (during coffee break), creating (as in a hobby), getting excited (at sports events) are features that God has given to the human beings he has created—laughter, friendship, creativity, excitement. Leisure is the enjoyment of the gifts. Our ministry is in the enjoyment of the gifts, because as we enjoy them, others enjoy them too.

We are performing a ministry when we make people feel valuable no matter what they are doing at the moment. When we laugh at their humor during coffee break and appreciate their interests in their hobbies, and share their excitement at a football game, we are multiplying the gifts God gives them.

Leisure Is Grace

This chapter on leisure really should be read leisurely. Leisure is like happiness. When it is pursued, it vanishes. The harder one works at leisure, the less leisure one has.

Leisure sometimes becomes a victim of leisure. The recreation and relaxation can become so intense that we end up with the very anxiety the leisure was designed to relieve. Either that or the leisure time can become so empty of meaning that it leads to the very boredom it was designed to relieve.

Our English word "leisure" comes from the French *loisir* and the Latin *licere,* both of which have the root meaning "to be permitted," "to be free." The nuances of the word point toward "the absence of restraint or coercion," and thus the concept of freedom is central to the understanding of leisure. Not free time, or freedom from work, but simply freedom.

Leisure is therefore the sense of freedom which experiences all of living as being at rest and peace with God, self, and others. It is essentially spiritual as well as social and economic. Gordon Dahl suggests that leisure should be discussed as free spirit rather than free time.

Perhaps the adverb "leisurely" conveys more accurately than the noun "leisure" the way of living that is the goal of the Christian. Christians need not be ruled by the constant tempo of efficiency or by the tension of hurrying and rushing. To experience the rhythm of God's grace in all parts of one's life, even in the midst of energetic activity, is the experience of true leisure.

The bored, the tense and anxious workaholics, the person with shorter working hours and longer vacations, the retired, and all of us who get all tangled up in our misunderstandings and misuses of time know our need for grace. Leisure is a way God can liberate us from our strivings after idols of success. The gospel frees us from the tyranny of sin and death, but it also frees us from the tyranny of worldly commitments. It opens to us the walk of peace in the presence of grace. We live in leisure and serenity, composed in Christ. Christ is the Lord of our freedom, else anarchy and aimlessness reign.

Instead of racing frantically in pursuit of a good time and filling empty hours with deliberate activity, we may rest in the rhythm of acting and reflecting, giving and receiving. "I have learned, in whatever state I am, to be content," Paul wrote (Phil. 4:11), not meaning that he had passively submitted to circumstance, but that he had found a peace in all of his living. Such peace means a fullness of joy, so that our own activities are not exalted to ultimate dreariness. Augustine caught the vision at the beginning of his *Confessions:* "Thou hast made us for Thyself, and the heart of man is restless until it finds its rest in Thee."

We perform a ministry of grace simply by living leisurely.

To Live Leisurely Is to See
Life Whole

To live leisurely in an age of anxiety is not only to be a witness to the gift of grace from Jesus Christ but also to serve others. "I came," said Jesus, "that [you] may have life, and have it abundantly" (John 10:10). This abundance is not necessarily in wealth and things, but in rich experiences, mutual help and sacrifice, and sacrifice to Jesus Christ and those around us. Our responses to God's abundant grace and the gift of freedom in our lives are the clearest way we reveal our actions to others. If our living is completely hectic and anxious, we are not testifying to the presence of Jesus Christ in our lives, nor are we in a position to minister to others.

To live leisurely, to be at rest at the center of our being, amid the many frustrations and difficulties all of us confront, is to possess the wholeness and unity which comes from the gift of grace within us. The presence of Christ integrates our fragmented lives and provides harmony in the discordant world. This grace is contagious and puts others at ease. That is the ministry of it.

So leisure becomes a matter of attitude toward oneself, toward one's neighbor, toward God. Our ministry in the arena of leisure is living our lives totally in the here and now but at the same time in the light of eternity. A Christian is one who cares but is carefree. To pursue such a purpose, and each of us fails again and again, is to speak directly to the needs of those around us who have lost themselves in possessions or are frantically rushing after immediate pleasures. Tertullian wrote in the third century, "Sunday we give to joy." Christians may well say, "Each day we give to joy." Our ministry is to be glad. "This is the day which the Lord has made; let us rejoice and be glad in it" (Ps. 118:24). That is indeed living leisurely.

9

Community

LET ME BEGIN by having you meet two persons.

First, Greta, age sixty-four, who is a widow living on the edge of a small town in western Missouri, tells about her way of life:

"Twenty-five kids went to school where I went. Eight of them still live in town here. Life has been good to me. We lived on a farm until my husband died. I still grow and can enough food to keep me going through most winters. With my wood stove and all, I could get by for a month if I had to, if snow and cold kept me out of touch with the neighbors. We've always lived independent and I don't get very excited about government and world news and all that."

Tyson, age thirty-four, a designer of dental equipment, gives his biography:

"My high school had four thousand students and I don't know where a one of them is today. College was worse—forty thousand. My job could be terminated overnight and I wouldn't know until the radio told me what had happened to the company, but for now at least the orders for dental equipment keep coming in; at least I think they do, that is a different department.

"I keep up with the news—I have ideas on what the president ought to do in South America and who they ought to hire as coach for the new expansion team, but I don't even know who writes the contracts for our department or how the budget is fixed. None of that gets close to what I'll be doing tomorrow. The system is so complex. I'm just so dependent for tomorrow's food, heat, light, TV entertainment, even medical care, and certainly tomorrow's paycheck—all big systems; they don't know me and I don't know them."

Response to Change

We cannot ignore the changes that have taken place in our society. Our lives are dependent on institutions and organizations. They shape our values. That wasn't true a generation ago. As recently as World War II, most physical and material needs were provided by direct person-to-person relationships and family businesses such as the corner grocery store. In less than a lifetime, our living has become dramatically interdependent and complex. We are members of many communities, from neighborhood to global. We are now a society of structures, often impersonal and temporary.

We have all seen the change in educational institutions, for example. Most city schools before World War II were neighborhood schools, and many of the schools in rural areas were one-room and two-room buildings. Consolidation was begun in the 1930s and completed in the 1950s. Now, instead of teachers and parents knowing one another personally, most see the other, if at all, only during parent-teacher conferences. Our attitudes are colored by the lack of opportunity to be involved effectively in the educational institution.

The point here is not that we must or can return to a past time, but that in the light of changes in social structures, our ministry has had to change though the need for it has continued.

The number and size of the structures in society are overwhelming. They give many people a sense of powerlessness. Business, government, education, mass media, and political organizations are all massive. We are tempted to condemn them for their bigness even though we know we can no longer get along without them. (Not many people can go back to heating their houses with wood cut by hand from their own backyard.) Organizations and institutions are today's ordered ways of serving us. They provide the goods and solve the problems of a complex society.

At the same time that we feel we are at the mercy of the giant structures, many of us also live and work with them. Like it or not, we are identified with them. It really makes little difference whether we accept this role or whether we personally agree with the institutions' policies; we are part of them, and those outside will not let us forget that. In brief, our lives are pervaded by the structures of society. They shape us; we shape them.

Think of institutional connections in which your life is lived. Geographical communities are important; for example, decisions about zoning in a township affect all the residents. But other communities are also influential: the medical community of your region, the scientific community as it shares information, the business community which is not limited to a certain area but consists of a network of relationships, and so on. Each of these structures is corporate (part of a body) and communal (having much in common). They have been called "neighborhoods" by Mark Gibbs and Ralph Morton, for these relationships are close and associative.

> A man's neighborhood has ceased to be a geographical area around which a line could be drawn. It is rather the total of relationships that a man chooses to recognize—all that part of life with which he is consciously in touch.[1]

Through modern communication and transportation, these authors suggest, our context is international. For our community is not only our neighborhood and township or city where personal relationships are dominant but also our state or province as well as nations and global society where justice and peace are to be of concern for our fellow human beings. Kierkegaard put it well: "If there are only two men, the other man is my neighbor; if there are millions, each one of these is my neighbor."[2]

Networks of Ministry

Our ministry is therefore found in many networks. We are consumers, and therefore we have responsibilities not only for our own use of resources but also for problems of energy and food distribution. We are television watchers, and therefore we have responsibilities not only for our own viewing and that of our families but also toward the kind of programming that commercial and public networks bring into our homes. We are doctors, nurses, service personnel, laborers, teachers, business people. We have responsibilities not only as individuals but also within our jobs and within the institutions of which we are part. Our children and young people are in schools, and therefore we have responsibilities not only toward their particular achievements but also in the support of the quality of the educational institutions.

> The time has come to make the ministry of the laity explicit, visible and active in the world. The real battles of the faith today are being fought in factories, shops, offices, and farms, in political parties and government

agencies, in countless homes, in the press, radio and television, in the relationship of nations. Very often it is said that the Church should "go into these spheres"; but the fact is, that the Church is already in these spheres in the persons of its laity.[3]

These words, from the "Report on the Laity" at the Evanston Assembly of the World Council of Churches in 1954, remind us that we are already present in many spheres. We know the problems, sometimes all too well, and we know the people within these spheres. It is exactly at the intersection of concrete and specific relationships such as these that our ministry as God's people can be "explicit, visible and active." This is where the Word is translated to the world.

Thus it is the laity's distinctive task to be following up the mysterious, never entirely apparent work of the Lord in creation and in history. We are here where we can try to discern what the Lord may be about and to make that known throughout his body.

If the structures are serving society well, they should be supported and encouraged by our active involvement. If, however, they are structured in ways that keep us isolated, frustrated, or alienated, they must be changed. More important, all structures must be human-oriented. No matter how large or how important, structures must serve people, not vice versa. If the practices of an organization or institution enslave or decrease options for people, we can try to change them. As we are individually called to work for justice, so too are institutions and organizations.

Metropolitan Associates is an agency that did much work in the early 1970s in the area of Christian laypersons effecting changes within institutions. It suggested some goals that might be used in evaluating the human dimension of particular structures:

"Human" institutions should—

1. Insure the provision of basic material needs for all people.
2. Support and facilitate a concern for wholeness in persons as well as in society.
3. Enable the creative development and expression of human resources.
4. Enable the maximum participation of all people in the decisions which affect them.
5. Foster cooperative interdependence.
6. Encourage a pluralism of cultural forms and life styles.
7. Foster an openness to the future which allows for the growth and change of people as well as institutions, themselves.[4]

Our Christian ministry to structures can take many forms, but what are some specific ways in which Christians have effected and could effect change within organizations and institutions?

Becoming Educated

We must understand and know the subject in order to make a judgment about whether change is needed. If a number of persons within a congregation agreed, for example, that each would become as knowledgeable as possible about an aspect of our social structure, the pooling of resources from one another would be invaluable. Then too, newsletters from local, state, and national ecumenical offices alert readers to issues and suggest Christian responses to them. Conferences, retreats, and workshops all aid in giving insight into the complexity of today's social institutions. The Lutheran Church in America has adopted a series of social statements on such topics as human rights, ecology, capital punishment, and economic justice, which are helpful in providing guidelines for thinking and reflection. Education of all kinds is a way to raise awareness, to change old attitudes, and to give new direction.

Direct Action from the Outside

Individual initiative. Letters, telegrams, and phone calls to legislators, the president of the United States, advertisers, school administrators, editors of newspapers and magazines, television network executives, and other key officials are often effective. It is impossible to be guaranteed that all such effort will be successful. But without such action, the effect would be still less. The influence of a single vote cannot be known until the results are in. The power of a letter, a telegram, or a phone call should not be underestimated.

Group effort. Christian laypersons may find that it makes sense to be active in local, state, or national groups that promote goals of justice and human concern. Organizations such as the League of Women Voters or Common Cause can be a means by which individuals may coordinate their efforts. Demonstrations and boycotts are more intensive efforts to place pressure on institutional leadership to be more sensitive to moral concerns. Whatever the method, Christians should give careful scrutiny to both the goals and the means of achieving the goals.

Individual or Group Action from the Inside

Organizations and institutions consist of persons. By themselves, organizations and institutions can do nothing. Persons decide, plan, and act. And these persons are like you and me, perhaps *are* you and me. The very fact that Christians are already within organizations and institutions is a challenge and an opportunity. Such persons, working in a cell-like way (starting small and gradually spreading the idea), can and do affect the inner workings of all of these structures perhaps more than pronouncements from the groups operating from within the church.

What is necessary is to equip and support Christian laymen and laywomen for effecting changes inside the organizations and institutions of which they are a part. As Christians, we are called to seek and obey God's will in all our institutional involvements, and to enable change or resist change in such a way that all his people are served according to his will.

Two persons standing near a swiftly moving river suddenly saw someone floating down the stream and desperately waving her arms. Immediately, one of the persons on the shore rushed to rescue the obviously drowning individual. As he dove in, another person in the same desperate condition floated into view. The second person on shore jumped in to save this victim. Just as both rescuers came back onto land with the rescued in tow, yet another person appeared in the river, again in imminent danger of drowning. As one of the rescuers began running along the edge upstream, his companion shouted: "Aren't you going to save him?" The first shouted back: "I want to find out what's going on up there and whether somebody is pushing them in!"

A part of our ministry can be to determine causes. While we can continue to be concerned about individuals who need ministry—pregnant teenagers, alcoholics, drug victims, divorced persons, and all others in need—we can become aware of the social structures out of which such problems come. What kind of sex education is taking place within the schools? Why does boredom on the job lead to drinking? What causes the unemployment in cities which tends to encourage youths to use drugs to fill the vacuum? How do present requirements for marriage and divorce affect the high percentage of divorces?

God acts in history. That is one of the major affirmations of biblical faith. That means God acts in organizations and institutions. As co-workers with Christ, with a posture of servanthood, we must minister to and within the structures of society.

The Prophet in Society

What is frequently most needed in our various communities—large and small—is a prophet. We often think of a prophet as one who predicts future events, but this is only one of the characteristics of a prophet. A prophet is one who sees (often called a seer) and then speaks. A prophet is given the gift to see through surface appearances and point out the true situation. God sent Moses to Pharaoh, Nathan to David, Elijah to Ahab, Isaiah to Hezekiah, and his own Son to all people. All of these prophets saw through their society. They not only saw with their eyes but they perceived with their whole being. They anguished.

We have prophets among us in the twentieth century, just as the Hebrews had before Christ. They hear the Word of the Lord a bit more plainly, see the problems of people a bit more quickly, and speak out. Such speaking will be, as it was in the biblical setting, in the form of words of salvation and of judgment.

All of us have some prophetic gifts and responsibilities. In our role as twentieth-century believers, our concern is for anyone or any group of people for whom salvation is not real. As prophets, we are to announce judgment to those who have used their power irresponsibly. and to convey promise to those who have lost all hope. Having heard the Word of the Lord and seen the need, a prophet, whether Amos in Bethel or you and I in our communities, speaks clearly and forthrightly.

To Be a Prophet: To See and to Speak

The prophetic function has always been important in the community of faith. In the Old Testament, Samuel, Elijah, Isaiah, Micah, and many others were called by God for special tasks. In the New Testament, Jesus Christ, by becoming the fulfillment of prophecy, opened this role to all of his followers.

The biblical prophets all possessed absolute assurance that God had called them personally into his service. The root of the Hebrew word for "prophet," *nabi,* means "the one who is called." Frequently, the prophets were amazed and somewhat reluctant to be chosen for such an awesome task. The opening sections of many of the prophetic books of the Old Testament portray how the prophets received the call to be instruments to convey the Word of the Lord. The prophets more often than not tried to get the kings as well as the people to do justice.

But how can we, as prophets, know that what we have to say is God's will? If we begin to think we speak for God, our egos could run away with themselves. We could become dangerous. Maybe, but actually the greater danger is on the other side. There are more people who hesitate to speak out for God than there are those who speak out too much.

The prophets really did not want to be called to speak for God, because the call always meant the danger of being killed. The message of God is usually unpopular with the kings and unpopular with the people. A person does not like to speak out for what is right if it causes trouble with the neighbors.

In one area a refugee organization bought an old church building to renovate it for use by Vietnamese refugees. The refugees would come there to take classes in English, have parties at which they enjoyed their own foods, and share information about employment, medical care, and letters and news from home. But the neighbors were afraid to have people of oriental appearance in their neighborhood and they sued the refugee service to stop the proposed use of the church building. One of the neighbors, however, who was a Christian, got a call one day asking if she would help to persuade the neighbors to allow the refugees to use the building. She did not want to do it, because it would make her unpopular with the neighbors. Yet she knew that the refugees should have a chance to make good in their new land. That phone call was the call from God to her. She was not in danger of presuming too much authority in speaking up for God. She was in danger of not speaking up enough.

The prophet is sometimes stereotyped as a far-out wild-eyed fanatic who is antitraditional and highly individualistic; an activist. But the biblical prophets, from Abraham through Christ in his prophetic role, rose out of the religious community, identified with it, and challenged their listeners to live out the heritage from which they came. Instead of calling for radical new changes, the prophets usually called the listeners back to the fundamentals of godly living: obeying the Word of the

Lord, being faithful to the faithful God, treating everyone with justice, and being personally renewed once more. The prophets began their message with "Hear the Word of the Lord." They could be sure it was the message of God, not because they had heard a new message, but because they were repeating the same old message—"Do justly and walk humbly with God."

To Be a Prophet, to Be a Priest: To See and to Serve

Two teachers went into their laboratory to experiment. They called unto themselves forty young male seminarians and asked them to prepare a brief talk on a given text. Half of the young men were given a text on job opportunities; the other half were given the parable of the Good Samaritan. After this they were told to go, one by one at fifteen-minute intervals, to a building nearby to record their talks. One third of each group were told they could take their time to get to the building, one third that they had adequate time, and one third that they were already late and should hurry. But, behold, as each young man was on the way to the building, he saw a man lying in a doorway, coughing and groaning in obvious pain. Of the forty who passed by, sixteen stopped to help, twenty-three continued on their way, and, yea, one even stepped over the man in pain. When the teachers analyzed the matter, they found there was no relationship between the texts that were read and the persons who stopped. But, behold, two-thirds of those who were told to take their time stopped, while only one in ten of the late group stopped. And the forty young men asked, "What is the meaning of this parable, O teacher?" And the teacher replied: "Doubtless the priest and the Levite were in a rush, hurrying along with little black date books full of appointments and schedules and glancing furtively at each sundial as they went. But the Samaritan, being of much less stature and therefore unimpressed with his own stature, had few such appointments to keep. He truly was a neighbor; he saw the man, he stopped, and he made himself available at all times and places."

The language is mine, but the story itself is not. According to the *New York Times* of April 10, 1971, a psychologist and a theologian conducted this experiment at Princeton Theological Seminary.

The conclusion, regardless of whether the persons involved are seminarians, pastors, or laypeople, is modest but perhaps revealing. Instead of the usual explanation of apathy, dehumanization, fear of getting involved, and callousness, which are often cited in such situations, the point made here is that pressing concerns determined the response.

Compassion, serving others, whether in one's family or congregation, or where one works or with strangers, always has to begin with the ability to stop and to see. Before one serves, one must see the person, really see.

NOTES

1. Mark Gibbs and T. Ralph Morton, *God's Frozen People* (Philadelphia: Westminster Press, 1965), 86.

2. Søren Kierkegaard, *Works of Love,* translated by David M. Swenson and Lillian M. Swenson (Princeton: Princeton University Press, 1949), 18.

3. "Report on the Laity, Evanston Assembly," World Council of Churches, 1954.

4. "Report of the Lay Ministry Task Force of the Metropolitan Christian Council of Philadelphia," 1971, 34.

10

Church

WHERE IS St. John's Lutheran Church at 11:30 on Monday morning? Still at Fifth and Maple? Yes, but where is the church, the body of Christ, at that time? It is where the members of that body are: in offices, in kitchens, at sales meetings, in hospital rooms, at gas stations, in pastors' studies, in classrooms, on assembly lines, and so on. That is where the presence of Christ's body will be made known or will be hidden. That is where God will be working through persons, through members of his body.

Part Two began with the arena of ministry within our families and moved in larger, concentric circles through our occupations, and leisure, and our responsibility within the structures of society. It is appropriate therefore to conclude Part Two by focusing on the ministry within the family of faith, within the church, the congregation. A particular emphasis in this chapter will be on the relationship of pastor and people, between the ministry of the clergy and the ministry of the laity. Clearly, no brief study such as this can untangle all the historical and theological understandings of the role of the ordained clergy. Instead, the chapter will suggest some ways in which a healthy working of mutual ministry may take place within a congregation.

If you read magazines, you are probably familiar with tests to rate yourself on such topics as whether your marriage can be saved or whether you could live happily on Cape Cod on $100 thousand a year. A paper entitled ''All My Best Friends Are Ministers . . . And Some of Them Are Ordained,'' by Jean Hamilton, contained a true or false quiz.

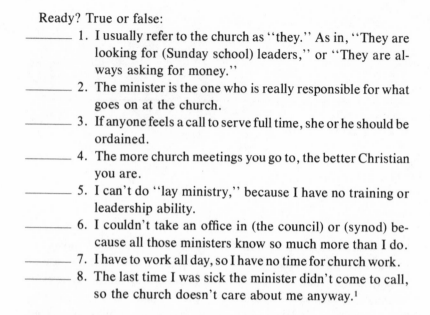

Ready? True or false:

_____ 1. I usually refer to the church as "they." As in, "They are
looking for (Sunday school) leaders," or "They are always asking for money."

_____ 2. The minister is the one who is really responsible for what
goes on at the church.

_____ 3. If anyone feels a call to serve full time, she or he should be
ordained.

_____ 4. The more church meetings you go to, the better Christian
you are.

_____ 5. I can't do "lay ministry," because I have no training or
leadership ability.

_____ 6. I couldn't take an office in (the council) or (synod) because all those ministers know so much more than I do.

_____ 7. I have to work all day, so I have no time for church work.

_____ 8. The last time I was sick the minister didn't come to call,
so the church doesn't care about me anyway.[1]

The quiz concluded that if you have marked even one true, you are
probably suffering from pastor-laity gap and should see your New
Testament at once.

Mutual Ministry

The church of Jesus Christ is not to be understood as a ladder with
clergy at the top and then full-time church workers, and at the bottom
the laity. Rather, the church is a circle, a fellowship indeed a body, a
community ministering to one another and together to the world.

Mutuality and interdependence are to be the marks of the church. A
partnership between clergy and laity is absolutely essential. Sometimes an unconscious conspiracy between clergy and laity produces a
bargain in which both parties agree to certain conditions in return for
particular rewards. One party (the clergy) is allowed to feel in charge
at the expense of feeling isolated and insecure. The other party (the
laity) is allowed to feel cared for and secure at the expense of feeling
slightly inferior and with less power.

A full and rich understanding of the ministry of the laity in no way
lowers the office of the ordained. I am not interested in lay lib, some
kind of distorted Americanism which says: We're all alike and no one
can tell me anything. If the ministry of the laity encourages that kind

of egalitarianism, then the church must respond in clear terms of rejection. The issue in all this is not one of worth and power and status, but that of calling and gifts and response and responsibility.

I know, as you may also, some clergy who still live "the Herr Pastor" role in dictatorial ways. And I also know lay persons who are obstreperous in their dealings with clergy. But much more frequent are the many clergy who are uncertain of their identity and lay persons who have great doubts about living out their faith.

At its worst, a church can be both clerical and anticlerical at the same time, failing to meet the actual needs of the laity but also failing to be supportive of the clergy.

Someone has compared health care and the ministry. Doctors and nurses are trained, approved, and employed in the health care profession. Yet the medical professionals cannot create health; they can only treat diseases. The professional ministry cannot create ministry; the laity have to recognize themselves as ministers and engage in ministry. We all practice health care. People trained in CPR use their skill to save the lives of heart attack victims. The family and friends of a victim provide care and support during and after the illness. The victim practices health care through proper diet and exercise. Health care involves all of these. And when that kind of mutual ministry is present, a congregation can be in ministry together to the world.

Did you ever go into an office whose only reason for existence was to serve, and find all the employees talking to one another, busy with their own small tasks, and no one came to the counter to find out your need? We may not be aware of how true a picture this is of the church in relation to the world. The only difference is that in the church, whoever does come to the counter will probably invite you to come inside, where some work will be found for you to do behind the counter.

Mutual ministry implies not only that clergy and laity work in partnership but that they see that the central mission of the church is to be in ministry together in the world.

Thus the question is: If the church is the salt or leaven within the world, how can the members of Christ's body minister to encourage and support one another?

The answer can begin with a discussion of some hindrances to the presence of a healthy relationship between the pastor and the people, and among the members:

JOHN JONES: Let the pastor do it all. After all, he's paid to witness, to call on the sick, and all the rest.

Through passivity and indifference and evasion, laypeople can ignore their opportunity to be the people of God, Christ's ministers within the world.

PASTOR SMITH: Since nobody around the church seems to want to do anything, I have to do it all: type the bulletins, run them off, visit all the sick, comfort the sorrowing, and put in endless hours of counseling.

The pastor, a Jack or Jill of all trades, either through presumption or because of a lack of lay response, takes on more and more responsibilities. He or she begins to feel like a firefighter who puts out conflagrations all over the place. Meanwhile, the pastor becomes the sole minister of the church, overworked, lonely, and frustrated.

MRS. MARY BROWN: Worship is between me and God. I sit by myself on Sunday morning, and I leave by myself.

To support and encourage one another as members of one body is a renewing part of our faith.

PASTOR BLACK: My purpose is to get everybody working for the church: distributing flowers, reading the lessons, perhaps even assisting with Communion.

Such intentions are certainly commendable; members of the body helping one another in service within the church. But sometimes this purpose leads to laypeople being seen as quasi-clergy, as assistant pastors. All energies are spent on maintaining the machinery of the parish. Pastors then find themselves constantly attempting to inject life into congregations, keeping committees and programs going, maintaining attendance and offerings. But ministry of the laity does not mean making laity look like clergy, teaching them how to pray in public, letting them read a lesson in church and preach once a year—though none of that is a bad idea. The ministry of the laity in its fullest sense means teaching and training and encouraging laypeople to be ministers of Christ and priests to one another within the context of their lives. The ministry of the laity also means working joyfully at being the body of Christ in the family, the neighborhood, the office or factory, the nation, the world; rejoicing at good things and caring for needs, wounds, and injustices because of the gospel; bringing skill and caring together in the life of the laity.

In order to support and encourage one another in ministry within the congregation, both pastor and laypeople might reexamine their roles.

The Ministry of the Pastor

The pastor is to be a servant of servants. This phrase, sometimes used by Pope John XXIII, meaningfully describes the great responsibility and calling of the pastor. Rather than an issue of power ("I as layperson want to have the same power as a pastor"; or, "I as clergy do not want laypeople in my parish to take over"), the entire context of ministry is one of service and mutuality. Recognizing the ministry of the laity is not a matter of the laity's desiring to share status and privilege, but rather a matter of the basic understanding of the nature of the church. As one layperson has said: "Ministry is not something clergy has, to be shared with laypeople at the clergy's will. Ministry is for all baptized people, and all share responsibility for it." As the body of Christ, the church exists "not to be served but to serve" (Matt. 20:28). In acknowledging lordship over its own life, the church is to be world-serving, not self-serving. And in that context the pastor is a servant of servants.

The pastor is to be the bearer of the office of Word and Sacrament. This function, and with it the directing of public worship, is central to the task of the pastor. But within this affirmation come further questions: What kind of preaching of the Word will best encourage and strengthen the ministries of this congregation? How may the essential meanings of Baptism and Communion stimulate the members in their ministry? What kind of worship, especially prayers, is helpful to the people of God as they continue their ministry this coming week? The pastor is to be the resident theologian, as one parish pastor has called it. The pastor's education, both past and continuing, is an invaluable resource both to instruct and to give direction to the members of the congregation. The pastor's awareness of the biblical and historical traditions may be needed to correct a distortion that a member is pursuing. Or, the resident theologian may attempt to share the vision of what it means to be an Amos or a Lydia or a Timothy in our day.

The pastor is to know the secular world, particularly the context of the parishioners' lives. The pastor must not be isolated from the needs of fellow believers. Home visiting brings a knowledge of life in the home, but visiting the place of work puts the pastor in touch with a different world. One pastor regularly visits the offices or factories where the men and women of the parish work or has lunch in the cafeterias or in the corporation's dining room as a guest. All of this is done so that pastors may acquire a knowledge of the conditions under which their laypeople live during the week.

The pastor is to be the enabler of ministry. Enablement refers to the process by which pastors, through instruction and encouragement, make it possible for others to fulfill the purposes of their lives. An enabler is someone who provides the climate for others to become the persons God intended them to be. An enabler affirms the efforts of others, yet lovingly provides correction when energies are poorly directed. One pastor calls the role one of weaving, of supporting and interconnecting the various strengths of the members. When a task is to be accomplished, for example, the pastor's question is primarily who could do this the best. But the pastor must also try to seek out those persons who are unattached members of the body (either new or inactive) who might grow closer to one another and to Christ as they together undertake the task. Another pastor uses a different approach. If asked to be a member of a community committee or organization, the pastor may request to be allowed to contact a layperson in the congregation to serve in this function. This pastor feels that a layperson frequently has more expertise in the subject and that the layperson may recognize more explicitly that this is a task of Christian ministry. Most of all, the pastor has enabled, has helped to make possible, the work of God on earth to go forward.

In brief, clergy are teachers who make the biblical word come alive with meaning and persuasion. They are priests who declare the mysteries of the sacraments. And they are pastors applying the oil of care and healing to our wounds, helping us to recover the courage to face each day's demands, and inspiring hope in the face of difficulties and failures. If they do their own work well, they prepare the laity to do its work well.

The Ministry of the People

The people are to encourage and support the pastor. Pastors are human beings and they have real needs. That should be self-evident, but from many pastors and their families one hears of feelings of loneliness and isolation. There is no more urgent ministry than a ministry to church leaders. To encourage and support them, to pray for them, to be in conversation with them if there are differences, to be a listener, to be a sounding board or a critic if the need arises—all these are ways in which laypersons can help their pastors. Laypersons frequently expect pastors to be hired plaster saints, to be model Christians. After all, as laypeople we can then have a little lower standard for ourselves. Pastors need more than an occasional comment from us as we shake hands at the end of the service. As individuals and as families, they need friends. They need people who *care* for them, who serve and love them in the name of Christ.

The people are to be open and responsive to the pastor. A pastor recently said to a friend of mine, Mark Gibbs, that he felt the laity preferred not to be called. Gibbs, who has worked in laity education for several decades, remarked:

> There is some truth there. The laity would rather not be called to a life of discipleship, which means facing up to the kind of thing going on in the world today.[2]

The passivity of pew sitting is still one of the greatest temptations for church members.

The stance of passivity has various causes: a docility which accepts the meaning of "lay" as second rate, as a lower status; an apathy which sees the church as a volunteer organization ("Lay ministry? I'm not into that!") rather than as an army whose members are already drafted by the mark of baptism; a lack of commitment to the power of the Christian faith which sees the church only as a comfort station.

What each of these causes of passivity has in common is that many laypersons, in Hendrik Kraemer's words, see themselves and are seen by others as objects, not as subjects and agents.[3] Too often the emphasis of the church is primarily on ministry *to* the laity rather than on ministry *of* the laity. Ministry to the laity implies that ministry is a set of skills certain professional people have who perform them on nonprofessionals. The result is listless resignation (someone has called it "a taming of the pew") and a spiritlessness which denies the living freshness of the Holy Spirit working within the body of Christ, who bestows all kinds of gifts among the people of God.

Ministry *to* the laity can be labeled and packaged. But ministry *of* the laity understands ministry more like an adverb than a noun, a thing. The servanthood which I have received from Christ influences the *way* I approach everything in my life. Ministry *of* the laity is a way of living in which attitudes, perceptions, and behaviors are informed by faith. To nurture ministry *of* the laity is what the task of the Christian community is about.

The congregation, as I shall try to indicate in chapter 12, can become a center for equipping one another for ministry. To make that happen takes an enabling pastor and a responsive laity. Just as a pastor should not feel threatened when a layperson speaks of the ministry of the laity, so a layperson should not assume that a pastor is shirking responsibility when he or she encourages lay ministry. Mutual trust and openness are prerequisites to ministry. True partnership between pastor and laypeople is a mighty force for the work of Christ in the world.

All of the members are called to minister, to build up the body of Christ. Quite obviously, the leaders themselves are part of the body and in need of upbuilding. This relationship is what makes ministry a dynamic function and produces growth within and without. Such a corporate ministry belongs to the whole body, every joint, each part. The church is not first of all a building or a concept; the church is a body, an organized unity together in Christ. We are interrelated and therefore interdependent. And like a healthy body, it must maintain itself by caring for its inner workings; but like a human being, the church finds its greatest meaning in giving itself to others in love and service. Just as Christ as the head of the church gave himself in living and sacrificial service to the world, so the living church finds its continued renewal by giving itself in love and service to one another and to the world.

NOTES

1. Adapted from Jean Hamilton, "All My Best Friends Are Ministers . . . And Some of Them Are Ordained," a paper published in 99 *Percenter,* Fall 1976, by the Episcopal Church Center, New York.
2. Mark Gibbs, "The Christian Laity Today," a paper (Audenshaw Document No. 67, 1977), published by the Audenshaw Foundation, Richmond, Yorkshire, England.
3. Hendrik Kraemer, *A Theology of the Laity* (London: Lutterworth Press, 1958), 18–19.

PART THREE

EQUIPPED AND SUPPORTED IN MINISTRY

11

The Inner and the Outer Journey

BISHOP J. A. T. ROBINSON, who wrote the best-selling book *Honest to God,* has suggested in a later work, *The New Reformation?* [1] that the new source for theology in our time is the laity. In the past, the sources have been the councils of the church, the monasteries, and the universities. They have produced episcopal theology (the bishops), monastic theology (the monks), and scholastic theology (the professors). More recently, since the nineteenth century, the seminaries have produced pastoral theology (the clergy). Bishop Robinson goes on to say that although all of these strands will continue to nourish the church as they have in the past, the creative source for the twentieth century is the *laos* in the world. The theology they will bring about will grow out of their lives in the world.

Our life in the world is the outer journey. In the outer journey of ministry, we struggle in all the arenas of our daily lives. The outer journey is often treacherous and difficult, and thus the inner journey within the self needs nurture and support. To venture farther in the midst of loneliness, frustration, and discouragement, renewal and refreshment are essential.

Our lives this past week and this coming week are part of our journey. What peaks and valleys will we encounter? What routes will the journey take? What unexpected turns will be before us?

For to see life as a journey is to ask fundamental questions: Where have I been? Where am I now? Where am I going?

Other questions we wrestle with are more specific:

—In what sense is the secular world the world that God so loved that he gave his Son?

—Is the modern world, in which we live and work, God's creation, and is the service we perform in it God's service?

—How does the Sunday world of worship and community relate to the Monday world of work and loneliness?

—What does the life, death, and resurrection of Jesus Christ have to do with all the arenas in which we live?

—How and when do I begin my ministry?

—If I am already in ministry, how may I increase its effectiveness? How do I give and receive support in my ministry?

—How do I become more purposeful and intentional about my service?

—Most of all, how do I grow in ministry?

Answers do not come instantly. They come gradually, as God enlightens us with the Word, nourishes us with the sacraments, and helps us work out our ministry in our particular circumstances. This chapter will discuss the way our ministry can be strengthened by the means of grace, guided by plans, and supported by others.

Means of Grace for Ministry

God strengthens us for our ministry through the Word and sacraments. The Word is Christ speaking to us through Scripture, friends, teachers, students, strangers. The sacraments are the Holy Spirit coming to adopt us in Baptism and Christ coming to be present with us in Communion.

The good news about this is that God comes to us from the outside. We don't have to qualify for ministry from within first. We don't have to develop talents or see visions with signs before we have God. He comes to us freely in natural ways, through conversations with people and through the signs of the sacraments.

The Word and the sacraments stem from the root of Christian ministry. Without such roots, the entire undertaking is apt to die of lack of spiritual nourishment. Disappointment and frustration set in. The Word comes to us at worship and in private Scripture-reading and prayer. The Sacrament of Holy Communion comes to us regularly, and our baptism can be remembered daily. These moments of refreshment are the "rivers of living water" which Jesus promised (John 7:38). Such communion is not an escape, but a way of charging or recharging the batteries needed in our daily lives. This spiritual grounding finds its sanction in the words of Paul:

Since you have accepted Christ Jesus as Lord, live in union with him. Keep your roots deep in him, build your lives on him, and become stronger in your faith, as you were taught. And be filled with thanksgiving. (Col. 2:6–7, TEV)

Christ makes us both spiritually alive and worldly active. Prayer and politics do mix. God talk and human talk aren't opposites. Contemplation and calculation aren't in conflict. Inner transformation is the work of God, but so is outer transformation.

Through the Word and the sacraments, we are strengthened for Christian ministry empowered by God's means of grace. If ministry is God's work through us, then the Word and the sacraments are the means by which our lives are made malleable for that purpose. Our strength comes not because we do something but because the Holy Spirit works in and through and with us. As God communes us, we are given a breather, given divine "re-Spiration." Thomas Aquinas had an even more evocative description of prayer: *Recreatio mentis in Deum,* the re-creation of the soul in God. Prayer, like breathing, is the lifeline within the rhythms of our living.

Not only do the Word and the sacraments strengthen, they are also an *encounter.* They cause us to encounter ourselves, others, and most of all God, as we hear the Word at worship and in our personal study and prayer. Perhaps that is one of the reasons we are rather reluctant to bring prayer into our daily lives. Sometimes we fear being thought pious or we do not see the effect of prayer, but more often we sense that prayer raises questions which we prefer to leave unasked. To pray is to enter areas concerning our personal relationships and the meaning of our love. Prayer speaks of forgiveness, a word that seems easier to use in a building set apart for worship than in an office or a kitchen or a gas station. But that is exactly where communion and communication with God are sometimes most needed. "We should desire and engage in prayer," wrote St. Teresa in the sixteenth century, "not for our enjoyment, but for the sake of acquiring this strength which fits us for service."[2] Prayer, as ministry itself, begins with who and where we are. Into these very encounters comes the sense of thankfulness, intercession, and forgiveness which God's Word expresses. Even the distractions and mind wandering we experience as we pray can be acknowledged by incorporating these matters into our prayers. Whatever we encounter in all our living becomes the base on which our praying takes place.

The Word and the sacraments *prepare* us to be ourselves for our ministry each day. The Iona Community, located in Britain, uses the phrase "the plotted day." When we begin each day, we can try to anticipate the events of the day and "remember our baptism," as Luther said. The Word coming to us in Scripture and prayer can make seemingly mundane happenings into purposeful ministry. The Word can also help us know that God is still noticing us even when we have endless hours of meaningless routine.

And the Word and the sacraments bring *recollection*. At the end of a day or a week or a year, our scattered fragments are gathered by God and given meaning. As God's ministry brings us recollections, then we are led to be grateful and to want to intercede for others. The need for forgiveness will surface in our prayers. As we begin and end the day within the means of grace, and in between have times of explicit or implicit communication with God, we find our ministry more related to God.

We may read Scripture to increase our biblical knowledge or to feed our worship life. Either way, Scripture-reading begins with the expectation that the Spirit who inspired the writers of old can claim the words of the Bible again and make them the Word for us. The Bible is a mirror in which our own lives are reflected. We hear the question to Adam: Where are you? We wrestle with Jacob's God, we hear the still small voice speaking to Elijah. We speak through each of the persons who came to Jesus in their need. The Bible is written by persons for persons. Although our customs and clothing differ in the twentieth century from those in Bible times, our elementary human strengths and frailties are similar to those of Moses (impatience), David (forgetful of God), and Peter (denying of Christ). Therefore, in any ministry, we can and do identify with those persons in our Bibles.

Some find that the Psalms or Proverbs speak most to them; others respond to the Gospel of John or the epistles. No matter what the choice, a definite plan should be followed. The plan could include regular Communion, Scripture-reading, prayer, reflection on baptism, and most of all, sticking to the plan in spite of moods. Therein lies the discipline. We need God's grace most at those times when we have closed ourselves to him and others. The means of grace keep our lives in condition for the stresses and strains of ministry. Ministry takes vigor and a certain sense of self-control given by the Spirit.

But at the same time, just as in athletics, a relaxing is sometimes needed. For Christ to work within us, we must be open and a little loose. "Be still and know that I am God" is an invitation and command to listen, to be silent, to allow the center of our selves to become receptive to the way God is present in our ministry. Our inner selves, parched and dry, will then be filled by streams of life-renewing water.

Strategy for Ministry

In our ministry we are frequently overwhelmed by too many needs and pressures or by not seeing exactly where and how to begin. Without focus, a place to begin, or a place on which to build, our energies are diffused and are finally lost. Most of us plan ahead in our business or daily life, but do not even think about this in our ministry. Our skills can be applied more efficiently if we have planned.

We owe it to ourselves, to others, and to God to think through our priorities in ministry—what is really important, what comes first, what comes second. Specific goals that are realistic, tangible, and yet challenging should take into account our individual strengths and limitations. Most of all, such strategy for ministry does not leave out the element of faith, of God's presence not only in our successes but also in our failures.

A specific question may help: What target(s) has the highest priority for my ministry: my job, my working in the local chamber of commerce, my brother, the school system, or something else?

A method by which to focus on one's ministry has been developed by Andrew J. White of Lutheran Theological Seminary in Philadelphia.[3] The following worksheet, adapted from the work of Professor White, is for your use:

1. One of my ministries is . . .
2. The way I would describe this ministry is . . .
3. What I like about this ministry is . . .
4. One obstacle or risk is . . .
5. I might deal with this obstacle or risk by . . .
6. Resources I will need are . . . and I will find them by . . .
7. Something I would like to accomplish in this ministry is . . .
8. A first step to take to accomplish this goal is . . .

As we develop plans, we must be aware that a ministry in Christ does not manipulate people. Ministry is not something done to people.

Rather, it works with and through others. To map out a journey for one's ministry is to figure out what the goal is, and what are the best means to arrive at that goal.

Support for Ministry

The most important support is the presence of God in one's life—the trust that God cares about what you and I do each day. This trust frees a person to risk the possible loss of approval or status, and it also frees a person from depending totally on self, other people, and institutions for security. The belief in God's presence gives importance to what one does for and with other people. In such trust, a person has both a transcendent place in God's trust and a here-and-now place in this world, and out of that relationship acts responsibly as a minister of Christ.

Some questions haunt all of us: Did I make the right decision? Did I do the right thing? Is it good enough? But the search for perfection is self-destructive; the resulting guilt is overwhelming. At a recent five-week seminar on Faith and Daily Life attended by a dozen corporate executives, questions such as these were submitted in writing at the end of the first session: "Doesn't adherence to Christ's teaching preordain continuous frustration?" and "Does the church really understand that I 'must' make 'unchristian' choices at work?"

Christians need to remind one another that they are not required to be successful, but to be faithful. Faithfulness implies a stick-to-itiveness, or, in the old phrase, a perseverance in the faith. And one can forgive others and self because God first of all forgives our mistakes and pride and wrong decisions and all else. Forgiveness is not an abstract doctrine or rite, but a tangible and concrete need for imperfect Christians who are wrestling in their daily lives to live the faith they confess.

At a retreat weekend with other Christians, I met a person who had ruined his life through alcohol. His business was lost; his family had left him. But through Alcoholics Anonymous he was beginning to recognize the grace of God within his life. His question to himself and to us was, "What has God done for you this past week?" He was now more conscious of God's gracious presence involving all of his life. God's grace was not limited to certain times and places, such as prayer and church buildings. The undeserved love of God also showed itself to him in such experiences as laughing, crying, being listened to, being touched, loving and being loved.

God ministers to us in the ordinary relationships in the world around us as well as in the most unexpected moments through the most unlikely people. God's presence is real.

A second supportive belief is that many others have walked the journey of faith before. That is the power of Hebrews 11, that pantheon of faithful pilgrims: By faith Abraham and Sarah and Isaac and Jacob and Moses, and time would fail me to tell of . . . Such a procession inspires each of us to say, in the words of Heb. 12:1: "Therefore, since we are surrounded by so great a cloud of witnesses, let us also lay aside every weight, and sin which clings so closely, and let us run with perseverance the race that is set before us."

A Lutheran church in the Midwest has inscribed this verse near the ceiling in its circular worship sanctuary. Following the verse as it circles the sanctuary come the names of Adam, Eve, Abel, Noah, other Old Testament persons, then the New Testament disciples, early Christian believers, through the Reformers, and the more recent heroes of the faith, with Dietrich Bonhoeffer, if I recall correctly, as the last of the names. But what struck me still more was the space left in the circle at the end. This space affirmed that the journey of the Christian faith continues with new pilgrims in each time and place. And the members of that congregation, I hope, would have silently added each other's names to that circle of the community of faith.

But support is not only provided by persons from the past. It appears from a network of ministries of the laity presently at work in the world. To identify with others helps each of us to realize that although the Christian journey is almost always difficult, it is never impossible.

One such network is LAOS in Ministry which describes itself as—

A movement within the Lutheran Church in America which, through a supportive fellowship, seeks to help people identify, develop, and carry out their personal ministries in life.

The movement is based upon an understanding of ministry as a function of the priesthood of all believers—which involves every Christian in service to the neighbor through witness in word and deed—and an understanding of vocation—which in today's world occurs primarily in one's work, but which involves the totality of one's life.

The fellowship is open to all persons, who, hearing Christ's call to follow him, seek to find specific ways to affirm the Christian faith in all of their life situations. The movement does not seek to become a new organization, but rather a supportive fellowship which will help persons to be more effective ministers in all their relationships.

To be a part of this supportive fellowship, it is assumed that a person will accept, with serious intention, the disciplines of the fellowship.

a. The Discipline of Prayer—To pray every day, preferably at the beginning of the day.

b. The Discipline of Scripture Study—To follow a definite plan of Bible reading.

c. The Discipline of Worship—To participate regularly in the corporate worship of God.

d. The Discipline of Growth—To become a more effective minister through study and through participation in at least one enrichment retreat or conference each year.

e. The Discipline of Service—To identify one or more specific ministries in life and to allocate sufficient time to carry them out.

f. The Discipline of Giving—To allocate a definite portion of income to support Christ's work.

g. The Discipline of Love—To build a supportive relationship with one or more others with whom I come in daily contact.[4]

Small groups can be one of the main means of support for many Christians in their ministry in the world. Such groups consist of at least two persons but more likely four, and at most a dozen. They are formed out of the need that each of us has to be sustained within a community of faith. Small groups provide the sharing with companions as we carry on our journeys. Members of the group discover that others have the same concerns, thus breaking the "I am alone" barrier. Members experience mutual corrections, contribute to one another's deepening of insights, and help each other to explore possible solutions to problems in ministry. They share frustrations, struggles, and failures, and therefore find renewal of courage and hope. They celebrate together when any of them has a breakthrough in the ministry of the world. Most of all, support groups are places where Christians care for one another. They are attempting to follow the description Paul gives about relationships among the baptized people of God:

God has so composed the body, giving the greater honor to the inferior part, that there may be no discord in the body, but that the members may have the same care for one another. If one member suffers, all suffer together; if one member is honored, all rejoice together. Now you are the body of Christ and individually members of it. (1 Cor. 12:24–27)

The images in the New Testament about the relationship of each believer to the community all emphasize that each part is in no way independent of the whole: the limb of the body, the stone in the temple, the branch on the vine. A limb is not alive except as part of a body, a vine cannot bear fruit without branches, and a temple does not exist without stones. All of the images presuppose an organic link between the individual and the whole.

By accepting one another in all of everyone's uncertainties, members are willing to open up hidden fears or burdens. Trust is high because members treat each other with respect. They assume responsibility for each other and therefore are both accountable and call each other to account for shared decisions. Failures and negative reactions must be acknowledged within the small-group fellowship, for no trust and support take place without open communication. The basic purpose of a small-group fellowship is not congeniality, but the personal growth in ministry of each member.

Edythe M. Daehling[5] has developed suggestions for the organization of support groups. Much of the material following has come from her work.

The kinds of support groups may be various. The listing is not exhaustive and may overlap in actual situations.

1. Occupation-oriented groups. A group of five or six laypersons in the same occupation may share their ministries in the world by meeting together once a week or once a month for breakfast. Or, such a fellowship may gather over an hour-long lunch at the place of work. An alternative approach would lead to a group of persons engaged in different occupations. Some groups may follow the example of a group of a dozen persons who, during a Lenten luncheon series, each shared for ten or fifteen minutes his or her unique problems and challenges in a personal way. The comments and questions afterward supported and encouraged the growth of ministry in the world.

2. Issue-oriented or task-oriented groups. Particular problems in a community may be faced by a group of Christians who meet regularly to understand the situation, to plan strategy, and then gain support for action. Such problems as housing, community-police relations, and

schools may be the focus for persons both within and outside the institution involved. Such a fellowship may want to set particular goals, and when these goals are met, the fellowship may conclude its meetings.

3. Family groups. Families can support one another. The group of which we are members consists of three families with children from ages ten to seventeen, one family with children married or in college, one young couple without children, and a single person. We meet once a month at five o'clock on Sunday evening in each other's homes. Activities planned by the host family usually include a devotional period geared to the wide range of persons, some physical activity in which all ages participate, and a simple meal. Sharing our ministries, sometimes with the entire group and more frequently in twos and threes, naturally takes place. Or a half dozen women may share their ministries as mothers by coming together occasionally for morning coffee, with or without their small children. Or a small number of fathers may do the same.

4. Prayer and Bible study groups. Support for ministry may be met best by some Christians in coming together regularly for prayer or Bible study or both. The study of a specific book of the Bible or the use of a thematic approach to Scripture serves the purpose of encouraging one another in ministry.

5. Support groups within a congregation. Perhaps some adult Christians from a congregation of people of varying backgrounds, using a paperbound book as a catalyst, could spend a Sunday evening each month in one another's homes. Some congregations, often with highly mobile members, have found ways to form small groups for almost all members of the congregation. Such a network strengthens the whole body of believers and links each person into the community of faith.

How does one start and continue a small support group? The place to begin is not with a group, but with a hunger or a thirst. If even one person feels the need for support in ministry, such a person inviting one or more to share such concerns is the beginning of a support group.

The meetings may be as informal or as structured as the group feels at home with. Some meetings begin or end with prayer, either individuals rotating one at a time or some persons volunteering sentence prayers such as, "Lord, help me to . . ." A brief word of Scripture may give focus to the time together. A leader, either the host or a person selected by consensus, is usually necessary in most fellowships. This is not to be a person who dominates, but one who guides and keeps the momentum of the meeting, and focuses the discussion. Some groups simply have one individual or more share answers to the questions: "How in the world are you doing?" Others may have one or more individuals talk five minutes or so on this question: "At what point and in what ways have my faith and my daily living intersected this past week?" This approach, used by an adult class that met on Sunday evenings began with two persons sharing their inner lives and outer lives of ministry. It extended two months, until almost all twenty had shared the difficulties and opportunities of their ministries.

There are no rules about small support groups, only suggestions. Anything tried should be evaluated by the total group, so that the group's process can be managed to meet the needs of the participants.

— Allow time for trust to build. Don't expect the small group to be perfect.

— Make clear, as early as possible, what the purpose is. Check with the group regularly to see whether that purpose is being achieved. If the group so desires, the purpose and format can be changed.

— Meet regularly, no less frequently than once a month. Stick to that time. Begin and end each meeting at the agreed-upon time.

— Before each meeting ends, know where and when the next meeting will be held and what will take place there.

— If you feel the need, explore the subject of group dynamics in the many helpful books that are available on this subject.

— Always arrange some time for sharing the good and the not-so-good things that have been happening in the ministry of the people in the fellowship.

— Persons cannot support one another in ministry unless they are hearing each other. Really listen to others.

— Above all, remember that the purpose of the small group is to help each other to be more effective in ministry by being supportive and encouraging. One group began each meeting by reiterating: We are here to sharpen one another's swords, not to use them on each other.

What a small support group is, and exactly how it functions, may vary, but support groups are as old as Christianity itself. Christ's calling of the Twelve was, in part, the gathering of a small group. The sending out of the disciples two by two, rather than individually, reflects the necessity of support as we journey in our ministries today. We repeat the statement each Sunday that we believe in the communion of the saints, and one tangible way of expressing that communion is through groups. The support group is the nurturing ground for skills.

Receiving the Word and the sacraments, focusing on a particular strategy for ministry, and finding support for ministry are means to nurture and develop our service to Christ to those around us.

NOTES

1. J. A. T. Robinson, *The New Reformation?* (Philadelphia: Westminster Press, 1965), 60–63.

2. St. Teresa of Avila, *Interior Castle,* translated by E. Allison Peers (Garden City, N.Y.: Doubleday & Co., 1961), 231.

3. Adapted from a plan developed by Andrew J. White, Lutheran Theological Seminary at Philadelphia, 7301 Germantown Ave., Philadelphia, Pa. 19119.

4. LAOS in Ministry, Division for Mission in North America, Lutheran Church in America, 231 Madison Ave., New York, N.Y. 10016.

5. Edythe M. Daehling, former Secretary for Specialized Learning Experiences. Lutheran Church Women, 2900 Queen Lane, Philadelphia, Pa. 19129.

12

The Congregation—
The Whole People of God
in Ministry

THE FAITHFUL CONGREGATION, said Luther, is "a fellowship of conversation and consolation." A congregation exists to support people, not to use them. The congregation, whether large or small, provides the base to equip and affirm the ministry of the laity in the world. Christians throughout the ages have always been reminded that they are persons who are the body of Christ in the world.

Obviously, the ministries within the Christian community should and will continue: visiting the sick, giving Christian education to the young, and all the rest. Such ministries keep us in touch with the love of Christ. But the emphasis is to be on nurture, not simply on maintenance. Some busy pastors and some active laypeople are so preoccupied with maintaining the programs that take place within the four walls of the church that they give too little attention to sustaining the ministries that take place out in the Monday through Saturday world.

The congregation contains all sorts and conditions of people from every arena of worldly activity. It has so many places into which its ministry can extend. A congregation has educated clergy and lay leadership. It has financial resources available. A congregation has all the basic elements needed in order to organize itself as a center to equip and affirm ministry. What is frequently required is a major redirecting of such resources.

The Flowering of Ministries with
the Christian Community

Ministries emerge from a Christian community that lives a rich spiritual life and that attempts to place itself in a stance of justice toward its neighborhood and the rest of the world. Someone has used the phrase "the flowering of ministries" to indicate that ministries are to be rooted in the nourishing soil of the Christian community. No flowering of ministries will take place unless there are communities where they can take root.

Some congregations have recognized this by placing on their Sunday bulletins or their outdoor bulletin boards the following:

MINISTERS: Every Member
PASTOR: David R. Fisher

THE MINISTERS OF ST. LUKE'S: All the Members
THE PASTOR OF ST. LUKE'S: John A. Heffner

MINISTERS: All the Members
ASSISTANT TO THE MINISTERS: Pastor R. Wheeler

Paul in the Epistle to the Ephesians gives the focus for a full and rich understanding of ministry. "And these were his gifts: some to be apostles, some prophets, and some evangelists, some pastors and teachers, to equip God's people (*laos*) for work in his service, to the building up of the body of Christ" (Eph. 4:11–12, NEB). The key word is "equip," which in its root form means to make ready, to fit for battle. Paul emphasizes that pastors and teachers are to equip others for their ministries, not to do the work for them. The task of the church's ministry is to equip one another so that all might live as Christ's servants in the world.

Even the word "minister" has changed both grammatically and theologically. In the Scriptures the word is a verb (a thing done); now it is understood as a noun (a person doing it). The verb "to minister" is defined thus: to give service, care, or aid. The noun "minister" is defined as one who is authorized to conduct religious worship; a clergyperson. This is a sharp distinction. What was originally a function of the Christian community became an office in the church. Ministry was originally the mandate and responsibility of all believers. The Epistle to the Hebrews speaks eloquently of the encouragement and help which members of Christ's body share with one another:

> Let us hold on firmly to the hope we profess, because we can trust God to keep his promise. Let us be concerned for one another, to help one another to show love and to do good. Let us not give up the habit of

meeting together, as some are doing. Instead, let us encourage one another all the more, since you see that the Day of the Lord is coming nearer. (Heb. 10:23–25, TEV)

To Encourage One Another

For many congregations, a major shift will have to take place in consciousness and use of resources in order to encourage one another and to become a community for equipping and affirming ministry. Instead of spending money on a carillon or windows, for example, the spending might better be on forums to discuss Christian service in the world of law, finance, education, or family. We need to redirect the well-intentioned gifts of those who love the church to projects of love for the world. The laity of the church have a right to expect support and training in their calling as witnesses in the world; and they have an obligation to respond.

Here is a sentence-starter exercise to help you gauge your parish's sustenance:

—One thing the pastor said that made a difference in my job was . . .

—One thing a church member said that made a difference the next week was . . .

—I recall a prayer at worship once that helped me get through a problem at home. It was . . .

—A line from the Scripture readings that I often recall when I am dealing with people is . . .

—I take Communion because . . .

How many of your answers were about the big issues of the world—peace in certain lands—and how many were about matters of personal concern to you in your everyday world? Many congregations do make a worthy effort to deal with the major world issues, such as the need for global peace or the need for justice in housing. Such issues, whether raised in sermons or in discussion groups, are important and do need to find their context within the Scriptures and Christian thinking. But what the laity need and want is a general strengthening for Christian living in their daily dilemmas.

As a friend of mine once wrote to me:

Sermons tend to be attempts to work theology into real life, while the listeners are living their lives wondering where the theology can get in. Churches and their councils too often worry about funding for the lights and the programs without dwelling on whether the programs shed light on the needs of the individuals in that congregation.

The concrete needs of the laity must be met. Perhaps Mollie Batten has supplied the best illustration for ministry of the laity. She says the laity is a force of paratroopers. We are at the supply depot on Sunday preparing to be dropped behind enemy lines on Monday.

Such a picture makes a radical difference. The worship, the preaching, and the education all add up to intense preparation. Everything needs to be done to have each of the troops in the best possible shape for the coming week.

The image of such equipment, of course, is not new. Paul describes each piece necessary for the follower of Christ:

> Finally, be strong in the Lord and in the strength of his might. Put on the whole armor of God, that you may be able to stand against the wiles of the devil. For we are not contending against flesh and blood, but against the principalities, against the powers, against the world rulers of this present darkness, against the spiritual hosts of wickedness in the heavenly places. Therefore take the whole armor of God, that you may be able to withstand in the evil day, and having done all, to stand. Stand therefore, having girded your loins with truth, and having put on the breastplate of righteousness, and having shod your feet with the equipment of the gospel of peace; besides all these, taking the shield of faith, with which you can quench all the flaming darts of the evil one. And take the helmet of salvation, and the sword of the Spirit, which is the word of God. Pray at all times in the Spirit, with all prayer and supplication. (Eph. 6:10–18)

In the battle of truth, righteousness, peace, and faith; on the commuter train, at the telephone, and in all the arenas of worldly activity—that is where the mission of the congregation must be evident. Thus the congregation in its worship, its education programs, its budgets, and in all its decision making and priority setting, must serve and support Christians.

Many of the specific examples in this chapter are from the experience of congregations that have asked the question: How might congregations equip and affirm the ministry of the laity so that they might be strong in the Lord and in the strength of his might?

Regular Worship

As the church in its worship speaks the Word, it can repeatedly illustrate how the Christian is already a minister of Christ in the world.

In sermons and prayers, thanksgiving can be made to God for ministry that is already going on. With or without the use of specific names, the sermon and the prayers relate the Word and the Spirit to the actual lives of those worshiping. Through such concrete and specific means, the congregation becomes a supportive environment in which the individual Christian grows in his or her calling and is willing to risk for the sake of Christ.

In Communion we can be reminded that the bread of a person's baking and the wine of a person's making are the elements by which we share the body and blood of Christ. We are part of the stuff of nature, and the supper of bread and wine sustains us. And in the broken bread and the poured wine, we can be reminded that we are tied not only to the suffering of Christ but also to the suffering of all the people for whom he died. In the Sacrament of Holy Communion we are brought back to that from which we often attempt to escape: the cruelty, the injustice, the pain that people inflict on one another. In Communion, therefore, we are bound to one another, to nature, and to the world of suffering around us, and all of this in Christ.

In the Sacrament of Baptism we can be taught that through the cleansing work of the Spirit we are made anew and are initiated into the ministry of the work of Christ on earth. Baptism is the mark of ordination for the *laos,* the people of God. When we share that happy occasion within our congregational worship, we are conscious of our own ministry as a member of the body of Christ.

In worship we gather together to be scattered once more. But the word of Jesus Christ is, "Go. Go ye into all the world." If we were to look for Christ in his ministry today, he would likely be found, not in a cathedral or seminary, but in the hustle and bustle of the streets or off in a municipality somewhere sharing himself with his followers. Our ongoing worship experiences that kind of commitment: to be servants of God for the sake of the world.

Special Worship

Some congregations have found concrete ways to create awareness of the ministry of the laity. The affirmation of the ministry of laypersons may be shown by holding a commissioning or sending-out service. Just as a congregation pledges its support for its council, or its Sunday school teachers, or others who work within the congregation by holding a brief service of commission, so the ministry in the world should be affirmed (e.g., the ministry of healing, the ministry of teaching, the ministry with one's hands). One congregation asked each member to bring to the altar on Labor Day Sunday an object symbolizing his or her daily task: a sheaf of wheat, a dishcloth, a red pencil, a dollar bill. Another congregation requested members to come to church on Labor Day Sunday in their work clothes, and within an appropriate worship service, affirmed their ministries in the Monday world.

Another way to provide support within the congregation is to participate in a litany of gratitude or in a service of dedication. An example of such a service is presented in the appendix. These suggestions and the programs planned in one's own congregation are means to equip and affirm, to pledge and build up, and to make us conscious of being sent as ministers into the arena of daily living.

Education

All believers are theologians as they reflect upon the gospel in their day-to-day life and seek to shape their lives in faithful obedience. Thus there is a need consciously to reestablish the local gathered community as a theologically reflecting body, with seminaries, theological schools, and institutes seen as supportive. At present we seem to view parishes as "consumers" of finished theological products, produced by seminaries. Clearly, not all believers are equally informed in their reflection, and many are simply uninformed or misinformed. A very high priority must be placed upon the education of the laity, so that laypersons might more adequately fulfill their calling as God's people in the church and in the world.

Several educational elements can be adapted and developed by the local congregation: nurturing personal faith and encouraging the function of small support groups (chapter 11). In addition, training in skills for the ministry of the laity is crucial:

Discerning. In every congregation are people who know what is going on in education, business, politics, and community affairs. Such people can, on both informal and more formal occasions, help the members of the congregation to see the needs and to evaluate the particular situation. By bringing out the competencies of the variety of members in a church, the congregation becomes a kind of school of ministry to one another.

Listening. To listen to another is to enter the other's feelings. Interactive listening accepts the other and wants to understand. It tests for accuracy ("Did I understand you to say?" "In other words . . .") and, at all times, respects the other. Sometimes interactive listening suspends judgment in order to hear carefully what is said and how it is being said. And it knows that many people begin by giving the frame of the picture and not the picture itself. Therefore, listening is patient and does not interrupt; it allows the other to speak openly and fully. Such counseling takes place in kitchens over coffee cups as well as in offices with fellow employees or in pastors' studies. Listening and listening well is what Christ did, and it is a gift and a skill which his followers are to develop and use in his service.

Deciding. A congregation must see that its members are trained and accustomed to making their own decisions and being accountable for their own actions in their public and private lives. Often the most difficult decision is how to decide. A Georgetown law professor has said that in his listening to about fifty years of Christian sermons there were about twenty-five hundred (all of them) which assumed that the problem of choosing between good and evil was difficult from the standpoint of willpower; that is, one knows what to do but doesn't have the strength to do it. However, his personal experience was that it was not a problem of willpower but of choice. He was always having to decide between two choices which were both bad and didn't know what to do.

One of the best ways that training in decision making takes place is through dialogue and discussion within small groups of the congregation. Within the teaching life of the church, concrete problems such as family breakdowns, the drifting of young people, crises, and boredom must be dealt with. If such matters never enter the dialogue and discussion of the members, a kind of schizophrenia takes place in which all the real problems are split off and the Christian develops two personalities, one for the church and one for the world. By actually talking about such problems, both support and training in decision making take place.

A series of questions such as the following might be helpful in beginning discussion about decision making and talking together with openness and Christian supportiveness:

—What is bothering you in your daily living?

—When and how is it bothering you?

—What have you done about it so far?

—What biblical and theological resources are available for you to use in solving the problem or in making a decision?

—Describe what you think would be the best solution to the problem.

—How might you take the first step in order to achieve that solution?

—How might other people and God's presence be helpful to you in this problem?

—In the past few years, has your faith played an increasing, decreasing, or unchanging part of your decision making?

The congregation may assist a ministry of the laity by working through existing groups in its educational program (e.g., an adult study group meeting on Sunday mornings). The congregation may, as three churches in close proximity did, plan a special seven-week series on the ministry of the laity. Each session of the series was held on a Sunday morning during the church school hour.Outside speakers as well as members of the congregations participated in the series, both as individuals and in panels.

Other congregations have found that a weekend retreat is the most effective way to build trust and openness and support. Eating and playing together, studying and praying with one another, whether at a camp or another inexpensive facility, provides an environment in which the members of the congregation begin to experience the sense of Christian community which one hour a week cannot convey.

Congregationwide Emphasis

Whether for a single Sunday or for a whole season, the local congregation needs to focus on the ministry of the laity so that this challenge and opportunity are made viable and explicit. Obviously, in many congregations such changes have not yet taken place, but some congregations have employed one or more of the following:

—Looking closely at the time of budget building in order to see what resources are available for equipping and affirming the ministry of the laity. What might be added to the budget, for example, to provide partial or full expenses for two persons to attend a training event, and then for these two to train a dozen members of the congregation?

—Modifying congregational reports and time and talent surveys to emphasize the ministry of God's people.

—Using the congregational newsletter to highlight ministries of the laity. These articles should not be written as if they are success stories, but as descriptions of the varieties of ministries, which would include failures.

—The approach of ''How in the world are you doing?'' with youth groups has opened up new avenues for discussion and action.

—A series of mini-messages, perhaps at three consecutive Sunday worship services, in which three members of the parish talk simply and directly about how each has been ministered to in the past week or month.

—Consider listing in the church directory the occupations of the congregational members and emphasizing that at the time a person is taken into the membership of the congregation the new member becomes part of the ministry of the church in each of the specific arenas of their daily living.

—Reassessing the understanding of stewardship in the congregation. Does it include not only monetary giving but also the using of gifts of ministry both in the church and in the world?

Many people do not participate as full persons in the church because they feel the congregation would not accept them if they did. But the church is exactly the caring community which, in Christ's name, is able to give strength and light and forgiveness for our anxieties and failures, for our joys and concerns. A congregation rooted in Jesus Christ is aware of the ever-present commitment which comes from the Spirit. Such a congregation is a counterculture, a supportive community which shapes itself so that the truth of the gospel is alive in all arenas of daily living.

A minister of Christ is fully in the world, but not of it. A minister of Christ is fully in the caring community, and totally of it. And in that interchange lies the difficulty and excitement of being a minister of Christ in the world.

13

The Way—
The Ministry of Jesus

LIFE IS a journey, it has been said. Although the metaphor has become almost a cliché, yet the particular uses human beings have made of it reflect who we think we are and where we think we are going. The metaphors we use reveal us.

Some say life is a rat race; others say it is a race set before us which is to be run with patience. Some say life is a treadmill, all motion and no progress; others understand it as the walk of the pilgrim to the Eternal City. Some see the journey as a wandering through the wilderness or a labyrinth; others speak of retraveling the road to Calvary and the cross.

The motivations for a journey range from fear to faith. To leave the past because it is a place of darkness and dismay and to travel into the future with anticipation, excitement, adventuresomeness, and hope—that is the pilgrim's progress. The terrain may consist of mountain peaks, difficult to ascend but frequently providing excellent perspectives; or it may consist of valleys, descending into the shadows but often the place of fertile greenness. Or, the pilgrim (root: *per,* "through," and *ager,* "country") may wander in the desert and the wilderness (even a turnpike stop is called an oasis) and become lost in a labyrinth.

Amid the many differences in emphasis in all of these comparisons, all agree that living is a process, a developing, a growing, a moving, a going on a way. A few mortals have now journeyed through space, but all human beings journey through time. All of us are on a way.

The Scriptures indicate that the early followers of Christ were called the people of the Way (Acts 9:2). They saw their religiousness not as just one aspect of life, but as a total view; it was the Way. By first looking briefly at the biblical descriptions of journey and at the ministry of Jesus Christ on earth, we will be able to see more clearly what it means to turn the journey into a ministry. Paul as well as the writer to the Hebrews described the life of the followers of Christ as participating in a race: possessing perseverance, having not yet arrived, encouraged by the presence of God, and looking ahead to the prize of the crown of righteousness (Phil. 3:12–14; 2 Tim. 4:7–8). Especially Heb. 12:1–2 stresses this note: "As for us, we have this large crowd of witnesses around us. So then . . . let us run with determination the race that lies before us. Let us keep our eyes fixed on Jesus, on whom our faith depends from beginning to end" (TEV).

A Biblical Journey

The Bible gives many descriptions of journeys, each of which illumines the way for twentieth-century pilgrims.

One of the results of the Fall is exile and displacement: "Therefore the Lord God sent him forth from the garden of Eden. . . . He drove out the man" (Gen. 3:23–24). The human race not only fell and therefore was down, but was thrust out, out of the place of harmony and peace and nearness to the Maker. Adam and Eve experienced homelessness; they were people without a country.

But God did not forsake his creatures. He fulfilled the covenant promise by providing a country. He commanded Abraham: "Go from your country and your kindred and your father's house to the land that I will show you" (Gen. 12:1). In faith, Abraham obeyed and began his journey.

Joseph, a descendant of Abraham and Sarah, was forced to journey to Egypt as a slave. In this foreign land he prospered, and eventually the people of God were reunited and made this land their home.

Then occurred the journey which is the central action of the work of God in the Old Testament: the exodus (root: *ex*, "out," and *hodos*, "way"). The Israelites were surrounded with the presence of God which was before and behind them in a cloud by day and a cloud of fire by night. And with the support of Moses, Joshua, and one another, they once more journeyed to the Promised Land.

But the rhythm again moved from hope to despair. The dominant image is that of a people caught in the struggle between following and neglecting the ways of God. The forty years of wandering, those years of lostness in the wilderness, happened because the people of God forgot where they came from. They had to be reminded of the beginning of their journey: "I am the Lord your God, who brought you out of the land of Egypt, out of the house of bondage" (Ex. 20:2). In each moment of their journey the Lord was caring for them: "For the Lord your God has blessed you in all the work of your hands; he knows your going through this great wilderness; these forty years the Lord your God has been with you; you have lacked nothing" (Deut. 2:7). In victory they crossed over Jordan and arrived in the land of milk and honey. Centuries later, the people of the exodus became the people of the exile. After a forced journey out of their homeland, the people returned to Jerusalem with joy. They were back on the way.

The New Testament begins with a series of journeys: Joseph and Mary to Bethlehem, the shepherds and Wise Men seeking the Christ-child, and once more Egypt becomes the destination for safety, as the holy family flees from Herod. Later, John the Baptist insists that he is to prepare the way of the Lord.

It is in the life of Jesus Christ on earth that the image of the journey reaches its fullest meaning. Equipped with the power of God and surrounded by his disciples, he journeys back and forth in the Land of Israel. His last journey on earth is the road to Golgotha, bearing a cross of wood, surrounded by mobs and a few of the faithful, yet knowing that even his Father forsook him. He descended into hell, and then with power and glory he both arose and later ascended. Out of these events come many journeys of his followers. The joyful journeys to tell others that he has indeed risen extend later into the missionary travels of Paul and Barnabas, Timothy and Silas, and all the others up to our own day who relay the message of salvation. On one of these journeys, your ancestors and mine first heard the good news.

To Follow Jesus Christ

As pilgrims on a journey of faith, you and I realize that our relationship to Christ is a process, a development, a growing in grace toward a goal with the help and support of others. The journey consists of running at times, crawling, walking, yet continuing, being picked up and carried, sliding off the path, sometimes falling backward, until one asks in desperation, as Thomas did, "How can we know the way?" (John 14:5).

One answer to that question is to look at the example of Jesus Christ in his ministry among us on earth. Our task is to continue the ministry of Jesus Christ on earth. Our inner and outer journey is to reflect the way of Christ. Christ's life of service and witness was a ministry of deed and word in which he identified himself with others in total commitment. He emptied himself in order to minister to human needs. He comforted the despairing and challenged the haughty. He forgave the sinner and cared for the lonely. His ministry was to the body, the mind, and the spirit, to the total personhood of those he encountered.

The scope of the ministry of Christ was both deep and wide. His twelve intimate friends, and within this circle the three beloved disciples, formed the core. Occasional hearers caught a glimpse of Christ's ministry in the Sermon on the Mount, in the crowds on the street, and on the hill of Golgotha. Even his adversaries, the Pharisees, were part of his ministry as he prodded and challenged them in their narrow-minded legalism.

Some people followed the way of Christ immediately; others needed to be reached. Zacchaeus, anxious and tense, waited up in the sycamore tree. Jesus spotted him, but rather than asking the little fellow to speak to him, generously shouted for all to hear: "Hurry down, Zacchaeus, because I must stay in your house today" (Luke 19:5, TEV). Zacchaeus needed to be reached, and the Lord extended himself.

That kind of grasping and enclosing others marked the pattern of Christ. It did not occur to him to stay up on the Mount of Transfiguration with Peter, James and John when down at the foot of the mountain was a boy in an epileptic fit who needed to be healed. Later, when the criminal beside Jesus on the cross said to Jesus, "Remember me," Jesus replied: "I promise you that today you will be in Paradise with me" (Luke 23:43, TEV). The love of Christ encompassed others, and he touched them by reaching out toward them.

To Serve in the Name
of Jesus Christ

In ministry we serve and witness in the name of him who is Lord and Savior of our lives. Service without witness is obscure. The recipient is helped but does not recognize the motive behind the help.

Witness without service is empty. The words spoken are authenticated by the context in they were uttered.

Those who have studied the work of the laity discover that many people do not give sufficient thought to why they are performing ministry. Motives such as these are sometimes reported: a desire for recognition, "someone has to do it," "I can't say no to the pastor," or a sense of personal satisfaction.

Motivation for ministry is nothing less than to offer our total lives in service in the name of Christ and in witness to the name of Christ. Such directions give both motivation and the encouragement for continuing our ministry.

A friend of mine told of a young lawyer in Minneapolis who was aggressively combating slum landlords who were abusing their poor tenants. When the lawyer was asked why he was pursuing this objective, the lawyer quickly replied, "I hate the bastards!" My friend discovered that six months later the lawyer had given up the job. His hatred was not enough to motivate him to keep going at the difficult job.

Jesus once made the concepts of ministry and motivation specific by speaking of giving "even a cup of cold water" in his name (Matt. 10:42). Such a ministry not only is to the oppressed of society but also takes place in every situation we meet.

In our complex society we are very interdependent. Thus in order for the intricate, almost invisible network of humanity to function, we must serve one another. Such pragmatic motivation must be enlarged to include our willingness to live for one another in God's love.

To Witness to the Name
of Jesus Christ

To witness is to give verbal testimony, to give evidence, to declare the presence of God in one's life. We do not save the world. Christ has done that. Our task is to share that fact and to tell one another what that truth means in our lives. We proclaim the good news by sharing what has happened for and to us. We are sent to tell that amazingly good news that God loves the world. And that love has its source in that we love God because he first loved us.

The witness to the name of Christ must be personal—not someone else's words, but our own. The person must be in the statement or the statement is dead. A seminary professor recently related that, in his first month of being a pastor many years ago, a parishioner whose husband had been killed in an auto accident asked him, "Is there eternal life?" The professor said that he began talking of what the Bible and the Lutheran confessions said about eternal life. The woman interrupted him: "Do *you* believe in eternal life?" Such directness confirms that the central message of Christian faith was incarnate in a body, that the personal and concrete Word was among us.

To tell as simply as one is able that Jesus Christ is the center and meaning of one's life is to engage in the ministry of witness. No special knowledge is needed in order to say where and how one's life in Jesus Christ makes a difference.

Such sharing encourages us as we journey on the way. There is no magic formula for Christian ministry, no step-by-step detailed map for each person's journey. Yet the answer to the earlier question that Thomas also asked, "How can we know the way?" is clear and straightforward. "I am the Way," replies Christ. And each of us can help remind one another: That's the Way it is. That's the Way it really is.

A Meditation:
Twentieth-Century Disciples

AND YOU have come from Worthington and Bloomington
          and from Hibbing and Edina
          and from Cannon Falls and Pelican Rapids.
What if you had come from communities of Christians
          from Corinth and Ephesus
          or from Philippi and Rome
          or from Colossae and Thessalonica?
Imagine for a moment that you are first-century Christians, first-century followers of Christ. There would be differences, of course: clothing, language, and, most obviously, means of transportation. But there would be basic similarities. Some would be rural people; most would be urban: shopkeepers, merchants, homemakers. There would be the young, the middle-aged, and the elderly. All would be coming, as you and I are, from the hustle and bustle of their daily lives. They would be persons such as you and I with joys, sorrows, loves, tensions, boredom, who couldn't sleep last night, who weigh too much, who laugh and who cry.

There would not be a lot of brilliant theologians or eloquent preachers among them, for almost all of them would be laypersons such as you and I, who cell-like were part of the society of that time. They saw themselves as salt of the earth and as leaven within the loaf. They gave of themselves, as salt and leaven do, for the sake of the faith. Most of those people are anonymous; they are called "people of the Way."

We do know, of course, the first followers of Christ by name. Matthew 10 gives the list:

118

And [Jesus] called to him his twelve disciples . . . First, Simon, who is called Peter, and Andrew his brother; James the son of Zebedee, and John his brother; Philip and Bartholomew; Thomas and Matthew the tax collector; James the son of Alphaeus, and Thaddaeus; Simon the Cananaean, and Judas Iscariot, who betrayed him. These twelve Jesus sent out . . .

You say your names are not Peter, John, or Bartholomew, or what's his name, Thaddaeus? You say you don't see yourself as one of the Twelve or even one of the Seventy later called by Jesus?

But you and I are the disciples of Jesus Christ in our day. You and I are called by his grace to do his work in the world.

A disciple is known, most of us would agree, by several characteristics: a willingness to obey, to serve, to learn, and, most of all, a willingness to follow.

But if we look more carefully at those first-century disciples, those characteristics are not very visible much of the time. They are a rather unimpressive lot, aren't they!

    several with the smell of fish still on their hands

    one a small-time bureaucrat, Tax Division

    another, can any good come out of that district?

    and another, oh, yes, what's his name?

They had little to offer:

    no money

    no prestige: none of them is listed in *Who's Who in Palestine,* Year 30 edition

They had little or no formal education.

What could ever become of this motley bunch?

And if one watches them in action:

    Some scolded mothers about their children's behavior.

    Others panicked during a sea storm.

    Still others had the audacity to seek seats of honor in heaven next to Jesus.

    Three breathed heavily and finally snored while Jesus shed bleeding tears.

    One denied he ever knew Jesus.

    All of them ran like little scared rabbits to escape the swords and staves of the riotous mob.

    No, only eleven ran. One stays. He kisses Jesus and then betrays him.

Later, one had a bad case of show-me-or-I-won't-believe-it attitude.

Our initial analysis seems correct; they are poor risks. We can see why Jesus said so often: "O ye of little faith"! What would ever become of them?

But the answer is: nothing less than the kingdom of God!

Through these frail and feeble people, the seeds of the kingdom were planted:

from doubt to amazing confession: "my Lord and my God!"

from cowardice and denial to "on this foundation, I will build my church."

You see, in spite of their weaknesses and inadequacies, they were chosen to be transformed. Jesus said: Follow me, and they did. They had a power and a strength not their own. Jesus Christ still wants people who are willing to have his power and love show through. They possessed the one thing needful—a willingness to be open to the way of Christ—and God could and did use each of them.

One more matter. That chapter, Matthew 10, is really the first conference on the ministry of the laity. It's an instruction manual on how to serve in the world:

I send you out as sheep among wolves.

He who does not take his cross and follow me is not worthy of me.

He who finds his life will lose it, and he who loses his life for my sake will find it.

That first conference on the ministry of the laity in the world had a huge agenda. Only one phrase from Matthew 10 we might keep in mind as a kind of summary of what was said to those in training for discipleship. Jesus left it for the very end, perhaps because it was so crucial:

And whoever gives one of these little ones a cup of cold water because he is a disciple, truly, I say to you, he shall not lose his reward.

Such instruction certainly has social and ethical implications for the oppressed around us. But it is also concrete in many other situations. All of us in our families and in our communities are to give cups of cold water to those around us.

Frequently, we do not give a cup of cold water, but instead throw cold water on someone's ideas. Or, we give someone a cup of hot water in anger. Perhaps, a cup of tepid water is offered, neither a supportive nor a constructive approach to someone else, just lukewarm.

A cup of cold water is to give what is needed to refresh one another as disciples in our journey.

I wasn't there either at the first conference on the ministry of the laity, but I took some notes:

Don't forget who you are—you and I are disciples, those who follow the Christ.

Don't forget what to do—you and I are to give cups of cold water in the name of Jesus Christ.

Go now, I think you and I are again ready to serve God and follow Christ in all our living.

For when Jesus Christ was among his first disciples, he once said:

I came not to be served, but to serve.

And he did serve, he didn't just talk about serving:

He washed dirty feet.

He rubbed saliva in swollen eyes.

He listened to the woman at the well and to countless others.

He ministered to those around them in all that he did.

And when he left this earth, his work of serving and ministering didn't end. He left it in our frail and feeble hands. He left it not just for people with pastor and missionary in front of their names. No, he put his ministry in the hands and lives of each of us: you and you and you and you and even I.

Each of us is his servant, his disciple, his minister.

That's the truth! That's the gospel truth!

A meditation presented at the concluding session of a weekend retreat on the ministry of the laity held in St. Paul, Minnesota.

Service of Affirmation of the Laity

INVITATION TO WORSHIP

LEADER: Now is the time to live,
      to come to the Father who creates us,
      to sing to the Lord who frees us,
      to dance with the Spirit who fills us.

RESPONSE: *Yes, now is the time!*

LEADER: The whole world joins us in praising God.

RESPONSE: *The sky thunders his presence*
       The earth sings in praise
       The sea swirls in expectation

LEADER: The whole world joins us in praising God.

RESPONSE: *Your people across oceans*
       Your people across this country
       Your people in this community
       Your people in this place
       All the people praise you

LEADER: We gather for worship.

RESPONSE: *To be strengthened by the spirit*
       To be the people of God

THE INVOCATION

In the name of the Father who has cared for our past
And the Son who makes right our future

And the Spirit who surprises our now
Let us worship!

HYMN 551 (LBW), 438 (SBH) "Joyful, Joyful We Adore Thee"

CONFESSION

Let us confess that we have often failed to minister to the needs of others . . . (Silence)

Let us confess that we have often failed to tell others about what we have found in our life with you . . . (Silence)

Let us confess that we have not fully used the gifts you have given us in service to the world . . . (Silence)

Let us confess that there are parts of our lives which are still not fully committed to you . . . (Silence)

The Lord our God forgives our sins. Let us look up and bask in his heavenly grace. We are accepted as sons and daughters in Christ. Let us share that gift by passing the peace to each other. ("The peace of the Lord be with you . . .")

PSALM 100 (TEV)

LEADER: Sing to the Lord, all the world!

RESPONSE: *Worship the Lord with joy;*
Come before him with happy songs!

LEADER: Never forget that the Lord is God.

RESPONSE: *He made us, and we belong to him;*
We are his people, we are his flock.

LEADER: Enter the Temple gates with thanksgiving;

RESPONSE: *Go into its courts with praise.*
Give thanks to him and praise him.

LEADER: The Lord is good;

RESPONSE: *His love is eternal*
And his faithfulness lasts forever.

EPISTLE

1 Peter 2:9–10 or Romans 12:1–8 or 1 Corinthians 12:4–30

GOSPEL

Luke 10:25–37 or Matthew 25:31–40

THE APOSTLES' CREED

HYMN 403 (LBW), 538 (SBH) "Lord, Speak to Us, That We May Speak"

SERMON OR MEDITATION

SERVICE OF AFFIRMATION OF THE LAITY

LEADER: Each of you is called by God to a particular time and place. As disciples, you are followers of Christ in serving in his world. As priest, you are ministering to the needs of your neighbor.

RESPONSE: *We affirm that we are called to be your disciples, to be your priests, to be your ministers.*

LEADER: Your ministry is to be the people of God at all times and in all places
—on Tuesday as you are in your kitchen or office
—on Thursday as you are in school or in the factory
—on Sunday as you worship
—on Wednesday as you shop
—on Saturday as you engage in recreation
—and on Monday and Friday as you go about your daily activities

RESPONSE: *We acknowledge the joy we share in our baptism and we commit ourselves to service in Christ's name.*

LEADER: Let us pray.

ALL: *Heavenly Father, you have blessed each of us with unique gifts. You have called each of us into specific vocations, involvements, and activities. We do now earnestly dedicate ourselves to a ministry through these commitments of time and ability, so that through them we may give witness to our faith in you and communicate your love to all with whom we come into contact. Bless, support, and empower our efforts to be your agents of reconciliation and love, and keep us steadfast in our commitment to serve you. We ask for the presence of your Holy Spirit in our lives to keep us faithful to our calling as ministers of our Lord Jesus Christ. Amen*

LEADER: I ask you now to accept certain disciplines to aid you in your ministry:

1. Be diligent in prayer, asking God to make you sensitive to where you can give witness to him.
2. Study the Scriptures regularly so that you may be drawn into an ever closer relationship with the Lord of life.
3. Participate regularly in corporate worship.
4. Determine to grow in your ministry through personal study and through other means in order to be equipped for the ministry.
5. Identify one or more specific ministries in which you will engage, and allow sufficient time to carry it out.
6. Give a definite portion of your income to support Christ's work.
7. Build a relationship of support with others who have also committed themselves to the ministry of Christ.

Do you desire to commit yourselves to these disciplines as an aid to your ministry?

RESPONSE: *Yes, by the help of God.*

OFFERING

Each participant makes a silent commitment to a specific ministry. In addition to this, participants may bring forward particular objects which show the commitment to be ministers of Christ in daily life.

PRAYER OF GRATITUDE

LEADER: Let us thank God for those persons who have responded to Christ's call to serve in both the church and the world.

RESPONSE: *Lord, we know that you call us to serve our neighbor in love, not only in the church but also in the world in which we live.*

LEADER: For those who minister to the sick as medical personnel, or through hospital visitation and volunteer work,

RESPONSE: *We give you thanks, O Lord.*

LEADER: For those who help with the education of our children, both salaried staff and volunteer aides,

RESPONSE: *We give you thanks, O Lord.*

LEADER: For those who are actively involved in the political process of our community, state, and nation,

RESPONSE: *We give you thanks, O Lord.*

LEADER: For those who work for social justice, fair housing, and equal opportunity for both sexes and all races,

RESPONSE: *We give you thanks, O Lord.*

LEADER: For those who visit the lonely and the shut-in, and for those who find time to listen to the troubled and distressed,

RESPONSE: *We give you thanks, O Lord.*

LEADER: For those who serve through Meals on Wheels and for those who offer counsel and support through walk-in centers or anonymously over the phone,

RESPONSE: *We give you thanks, O Lord.*

LEADER: For those who work to make our community a safe and pleasant place to live, such as engineers, bakers, contractors, architects, fire and police personnel,

RESPONSE: *We give you thanks, O Lord.*

LEADER: For those who work with our children and youth through scouting, tutorial programs, athletic groups, and teen centers,

RESPONSE: *We give you thanks, O Lord.*

LEADER: For all those who seek both to glorify you and to help their neighbor through their work,

RESPONSE: *We give you thanks, O Lord.*

LEADER: For those who serve as homemakers, providing care, nourishment, and a secure haven for families,

RESPONSE: *We give you thanks, O Lord.*

LEADER: For all those who labor and whose efforts are often unseen and unsung but who contribute so significantly to Christ's ministry in the world,

RESPONSE: *We give you thanks, O Lord.*

LEADER: We pray for all who labor without hope,
For all who labor without interest;
For those who have too little leisure,
For those who have too much leisure;
For those who are underpaid,
For those who pay small wages;
For those who cannot work,
For those who look in vain for work,

RESPONSE: *Work through us and help us always to work for you.*

LEADER: Let us thank God for the love we have experienced in Christ Jesus which motivates and empowers us to serve others in his name.

ALL: *O Lord, we recall the words of your Son when he said, "I came not to be served, but to serve." He saw our needs, and he ministered to us in love. We thank you for calling us to follow in his footsteps. We ask you to keep our eyes open to the possibilities around us and grant us the strength, courage, and the willingness to continue to serve Christ and all those around us.*

In Christ's name, we pray. Amen

COMMUNION (if desired)

BENEDICTION

Go forth filled with the power of the Holy Spirit.
Serve the Lord by serving the world.

HYMN 503 (LBW), 515 (SBH) "O Jesus, I Have Promised"

NOTE: This service was prepared by the author, who acknowledges with gratitude that several parts of the service were adapted from material used in a service at Ascension Lutheran Church of Towson, Md., and at a Kirkridge Retreat service led by Pastor Raymond Hartzell. Used by permission. Barbara Hanst, correspondent, Ascension Lutheran Church.